The
Healing
Kitchen

The Healing Kitchen

Vegetarian Cooking with Higher Awareness

DIKSHA MCCORD

Crystal Clarity Publishers
Nevada City, California

Printed in China

1 3 5 7 9 10 8 6 4 2

ISBN-13: 978-1-56589-295-8
ePub ISBN-13: 978-1-56589-556-0

Cover design, interior design, and layout
Tejindra Scott Tully

Library of Congress Cataloging-in-Publication Data

McCord, Diksha.
The healing kitchen : vegetarian cooking with higher awareness / Diksha McCord.
pages cm
Includes index.
ISBN 978-1-56589-295-8 (quality pbk. : alk. paper) --
ISBN 978-1-56589-556-0 (epub)
1. Vegetarian cooking. I. Title.

TX837.M47525 2015
641.5'636--dc23

2015010550

---

www.crystalclarity.com / 800.424.1055 / 530.478.7600

Contents

Part 4: *Specials*

Part 5: *Basic Recipes*

Part 6: *Appendices, and More*

NETTLE
Calcium Tea
6 parts Horsetail Grass
4 parts Comfrey Root
3 parts Oat Straw
1 part Lobelia
Drink 1 Tb x3 a day
BAY LEAVES
SEA SALT
MUSTARD
FENNEL
SAGE
DILL
THYME
BASIL
TUMERIC
CUMIN
CORIANDER
CINNAMON
CLOVES

Preface

In 1993 I moved to Ananda Village, a spiritual community in Northern California. For the next seven years I served in the kitchen of The Expanding Light, Ananda's yoga and meditation retreat facility.

During those years I developed a wide variety of meals that were light and nutritious, yet original and tasty. We wanted our retreat guests—vegetarians and non-vegetarians—to enjoy every meal and to feel satisfied by their vegetarian fare. We also wanted them to feel alert and energetic afterwards, so that their meals would enhance their practice of yoga and meditation.

Those years led to my first two cookbooks: *Global Kitchen* and *Vegetarian Cooking for Starters*. Because there was much that I didn't include in those cookbooks, in 2012 I led a team that created a yearlong, ninety-seven-episode, four-season, online cooking show. In these videos I show in detail how to prepare many different types of meals, with an eye toward eating appropriately for each season of the year. To learn more about the online series, visit http://www.expandinglight.org/online-learning/vegetarian-cooking/.

This book includes those recipes—the culmination of many years of testing and refining with the intent of delighting vegetarians and non-vegetarians alike. This book is designed to help you:

- Explore the creative possibilities of a plant-based diet, rich in all the nutrients you need for a healthy life.
- Feel satisfied with healthful eating.
- Cook delicious food filled with vitality: meals that are light, easy to digest, low in fat, and that fill the body with energy and strength.
- Discover recipes simple and easy enough for everyday eating.
- Attune to higher consciousness as you cook, so that you share vibrations of love and joy through your meals.

Whether you want to become a vegetarian or would just like to incorporate more plant-based dishes into your diet, you will benefit from this cookbook. As you try these simple recipes, you will learn how to prepare tasty, nourishing dishes and easily create balanced, satisfying, and healthy meals.

Acknowledgments

I want to offer special thanks to those who helped me create my online cooking course, which was the inspiration for this book:

Adrienne Yam, who helped me in more ways than I can name; Dave Bingham for videotaping and editing the cooking shows; Barbara Bingham for her great photography; Rachel Ebgi for makeup; Mary Weber for bringing her creativity and skills to the sets; and the many cooks who shared their recipes and cooked with me in the videos: Devi Novak, Koral Ilgun, Jake Fuentes, Maria McSweeney, Paean Lee, and David and Caitlin Eby. Also, thanks to the many volunteers from The Expanding Light's Karma Yoga program, who helped with chores throughout the filming of the meals.

And thanks to those who helped with the creation of this book: Anandi Cornell, Dayanand Salva, Prakash Van Cleave and Lakshman Heubert for editing; and Tejindra Scott Tully for book design.

Special thanks to my husband, Gyandev, for his unending support and patience during the creation of the online cooking show and of this cookbook.

Diksha's Journey to Vegetarianism

I grew up in Israel in a loving Conservative Jewish family. While my father worked, my mother stayed home to raise her five children and cook for the family. I remember that, as a child coming home from school, I could hardly wait to eat her fresh, nurturing meals.

I enjoyed helping my mother in the kitchen, especially during weekends and summer breaks. I learned from her simple, healthy ways of cooking grains, legumes, and vegetables, as well as how to use a pressure cooker. She gave me a foundation for how to cook simply and joyfully, as a service to one's family.

We ate a very healthy Mediterranean diet. During the week we ate mostly grains, legumes, nuts, seeds, lots of vegetables, and fruits—simple and mildly flavored. On the weekends our meals also included fish or chicken, and a tasty homemade dessert. We rarely ate out. I don't remember eating frozen or canned food until I left home when I was twenty.

Somehow I've always understood that food was meant to nurture and heal, never to be eaten simply for taste and entertainment. Even as a child, when offered chocolate, I would have only a tiny piece. At home, when we had ice cream, it was always served in a small bowl.

After I graduated from high school in 1976, I met a young woman who had lived in India for some years with her family. She introduced me to Hatha Yoga, meditation, and a vegetarian diet. I was so inspired by everything she shared that I decided to become a dedicated vegetarian immediately.

I eliminated all meat, fowl, and fish from my diet and ate more bread, cheese, and salads. After a short time, however, I started to feel weak and realized that my diet was not nourishing me properly. I needed to learn how to eat a balanced vegetarian diet, without any animal flesh foods.

I explored many types of vegetarian cooking: raw, vegan, fat-free, macrobiotic, vegetarian, and Ayurvedic. I mostly studied, taught, and experimented for myself. And I also observed a number of fine cooks during my travels around the world and while living in Israel, Japan, California, and at Ananda Village.

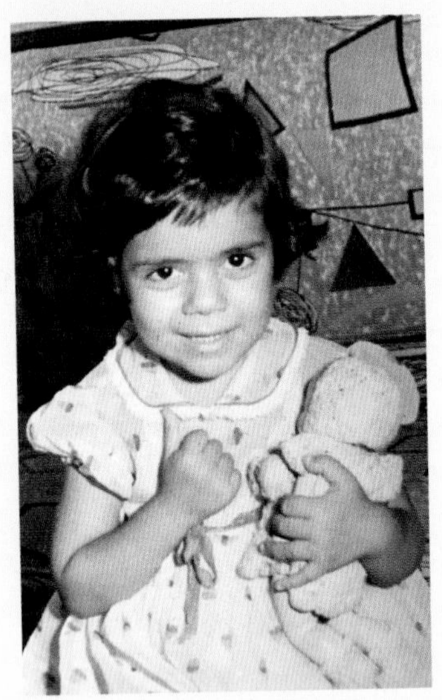

As I studied and experimented, I adopted healthier ways of eating. Drawing on my own experience of how various diets affected my health and well-being, I developed my own style of vegetarian cooking, which emphasizes the consciousness-raising qualities of natural foods, with attention to nutrition, delicious flavor, and appearance.

I use food as a divine source of healing and nourishment. For example, when I want to feel more grounded, I eat root vegetables with brown rice. I drink nettle tea to prevent pollen allergies. And I will drink green tea in the early morning to alleviate a headache.

My own experience has shown me that the more you eat what is right for you, the more attuned you become to your body's signals of what it needs.

When you are out of balance, you will crave foods that are not good for you. I hope this cookbook will provide you with delicious and satisfying recipes so that what you enjoy will also be nourishing for your body.

My best wishes for your perfect health,
Diksha

Spiritual Background

Ananda is a spiritual community based on the teachings of a great yoga master, Paramhansa Yogananda, and his direct disciple, Swami Kriyananda, who started Ananda Village in 1969. I have lived at Ananda since 1993 and have based this book on the teachings of Yogananda.

Swami Kriyananda

My deepest gratitude to my guru, Paramhansa Yogananda, for his divine wisdom and inner guidance. Swami Kriyananda (J. Donald Walters) was my spiritual teacher, friend, and guide. I am grateful to him for creating Ananda, an intentional community where people can grow closer to God; for establishing The Expanding Light Retreat, where guests learn the secrets of true happiness; and for inspiring me and many others to reach for the very highest in life.

Paramhansa Yogananda

The Expanding Light Retreat, Nevada City, California

Part 1: *Introduction*

- How to Use This Book
- Yoga and Food
- Spiritual Qualities of Foods
- Principles of a Vegetarian Diet
- How to Spiritualize Your Cooking
- Healthy Habits of Eating

How to Use This Book

This book includes six parts:

Part 1: The yogic approach to cooking and how to spiritualize your cooking. To gain the most from this book, read part 1 first.

Part 2: Guidelines for successful cooking, including the use of kitchen utensils, how to cook grains and legumes, and how to steam vegetables.

Part 3: Complete vegetarian meals. For each of the four seasons we've included eight complete meals, plus one or two special holiday meals.

Each meal includes all parts of a healthy vegetarian diet: vegetables, protein, and carbohydrates. In our online Vegetarian Cooking for Health and Vitality course, I demonstrate how to cook each meal.

Depending on your inclination, you can follow the book season by season, or experiment with different meals from different seasons. Cooking with a friend or family member will add fun and the motivation to continue. For variety, try recipes from part 4: Special Recipes and from part 5: Simple Individual Recipes. No matter how you use this book, you'll benefit from it.

Part 4: Special recipes for smoothies, healthy drinks, original tea blends, salads, desserts, and breads. The specials are also demonstrated in videos in our online Vegetarian Cooking for Health and Vitality course.

Part 5: Simple individual recipes such as those for breakfast cereals, grains, legumes, vegetables, sauces, and dressings.

Part 6: In the glossary section, you will find information about uncommon foods. Throughout the book, these special foods will be marked with an asterisk (*) to let you know you can learn more about them in the glossary. In part 6 you will also learn how to make ginger juice and ghee, and how to prepare for and do a nine-day cleansing diet.

Yoga and Food

According to the science of yoga, there is more to diet than just physical nutrition.

Yoga views all of life in terms of energy (*prana*) or "life force." Because we are sustained at all times by this life force, and because food is one of the vehicles through which energy is absorbed into the body, therefore, our diet should consist of foods that are easily converted into energy.

The more we choose to eat fresh foods, close to their original state, the more energy we will get from them. Natural foods—such as raw fruits, vegetables, nuts, and seeds—give energy to the body and calm the mind. Foods that are refined, processed, or preserved have lost their life force: instead of filling us with energy, they draw energy from the body to be digested.

> One third of what we eat keeps us alive;
> the other two-thirds keeps the doctors alive.
>
> —*Paramhansa Yogananda*

Life energy affects not only our physical body, but even more importantly, our consciousness. Consciousness is the essence of who we are; it determines our level of clarity, happiness, and inner peace, and our ability to concentrate and achieve our goals. Because our consciousness is also affected by the foods we eat, we need to choose foods that are rich in life force, foods that calm the nervous system and help to uplift our consciousness.

When you eat food, you are eating energy. Ask yourself: Is the energy I'm receiving from this food going to fill my body with life force? Is this food going to bring me greater peace and energy?

We are all seeking to be happy and avoid suffering. If food can help us do that, isn't it better to eat rightly?

The Three Gunas

All foods are considered by yogis to have an influence on people's mental and spiritual nature, as well as on their physical bodies. Some foods are said to be spiritualizing or elevating (express *sattwa guna*), some are activating (express *rajo guna*), and others are stultifying or darkening (express *tamo guna*).

Elevating Foods Sattwic foods include fresh fruits and vegetables, whole grains and legumes, fresh dairy products, nuts, and natural sweets such as honey, dates, and figs. These foods help uplift our consciousness, and promote vitality, strength, health, and mental clarity. They also help to calm the nervous system.

> Foods that promote longevity, vitality, endurance, health,
> a cheerful attitude, and a good appetite; that are pleasant-tasting,
> mildly flavored, nourishing, and agreeable to the body: such foods
> (give sattwic enjoyment and) are preferred by sattwic people.
>
> —*Bhagavad Gita (17:8)**

Activating Foods Rajasic (or activating) foods include cooked vegetables and fruits, onions, garlic, eggs, refined sugar, soft drinks and coffee, fish, chicken, and lamb. Foods that are excessively hot, bitter, sour, or salty are also included in this group.

Rajasic foods energize and stimulate our consciousness. These foods stimulate the senses and can create mental stress. They promote activating qualities: some of them desirable, such as creativity and ambition; some neutral, such as curiosity; and some undesirable, such as restlessness, impulsiveness, and aggression.

> Foods that are bitter, sour, heavily salted, excessively hot,
> pungent, sharp tasting, and burning (give rajasic enjoyment and)
> are those preferred by people of rajasic temperament.
> Such foods produce pain, discomfort, and disease.
>
> —*Bhagavad Gita (17:9)**

Darkening Foods Tamasic (or darkening) foods include moldy cheeses, alcoholic beverages, beef, veal, pork, dried meat, deep-fried food, excessively spicy foods, horseradish, overcooked food, and foods that are canned, overprocessed, chemically preserved, or fermented.

Tamasic foods darken our consciousness and make it heavy. These foods lead us toward dullness, laziness, negativity, anger, greed, jealousy, and inertia.

> Foods that are nutritionally worthless, tasteless, putrid, stale,
> thrown away as garbage, or (otherwise) impure
> (give tamasic enjoyment and) are preferred by tamasic people.
>
> —*Bhagavad Gita (17:10)**

* From *The Essence of the Bhagavad Gita: Explained by Paramhansa Yogananda, As remembered by Swami Kriyananda.*

The teachings of yoga recommend a diet that promotes harmony rather than stimulation—one that keeps the nervous system calm and peaceful, and fills the body with energy, vitality, and strength. By carefully choosing how we feed our bodies, we can influence and shape our minds and lives in positive, uplifting ways.

The Ideal Diet

Paramhansa Yogananda, a great master of yoga, recommended a diet that includes foods with both elevating *and* activating qualities. He recommended this combination in part because many people are unable to digest raw foods effectively. Also, because we live in a very active world and have responsibilities that require lots of physical energy and initiative. Activating foods help us to have the outward physical energy we need.

Yogananda suggested that we balance our need to fulfill our many outward responsibilities with the desire to seek a higher consciousness. Therefore, he recommended a diet that includes cooked whole grains, legumes, raw or lightly cooked vegetables, fruits, dairy products, nuts and seeds, and spices.

For a person in good health, Yogananda recommended a diet that includes 60 percent fruits and vegetables, 20 percent protein, and 20 percent starches. Such a diet helps us live a balanced life, maintain our worldly responsibilities, and meditate deeply.

Yogananda also emphasized the importance of a diet that keeps the body alkaline. When the body becomes acidic, the immune system is weakened and the body is more prone to disease. As much as possible, try to avoid acid-forming foods such as meat, coffee, sugar, and white flour products. Overwork, lack of exercise, and lack of fresh air also cause the body to become acidic. Eating an abundance of fruits and vegetables helps to keep the body alkaline.

There are six different tastes we can experience through foods: sweet, sour, salty, pungent, bitter, and astringent. An ideal diet also will *include all six tastes in every meal.* A meal that includes all six tastes feels balancing, and physically and emotionally satisfying.

Of these six tastes, only sweet is considered sattwic. Sour, salty, and pungent are rajasic; and bitter and astringent are tamasic. But too much sweet food can be tamasic, especially if it includes highly processed white sugar. Overeating any type of food can be tamasic. A sattwic diet is pleasant but evenly balanced in taste, containing some amount of all six tastes, and taken only in the amount necessary to fill three-fourths of the stomach.

Below are examples of foods with each of the different tastes. But it must be remembered that most foods have more than one taste, so this list is simplified, to give you an idea of what is meant by these tastes.

Sweet—grains (especially rice and wheat), some root vegetables (such as sweet potatoes), milk, butter, pasta, sugar, honey, dates, and many fruits

Sour—lemons, limes, grapefruit, sour fruits, cheese, yogurt, sour cream, vinegar, and other fermented foods

Salty—salt, seaweeds, and soy sauce/tamari

Pungent—radish, onion, garlic, and spices such as cayenne, chili, black pepper, mustard, ginger, and garlic

Bitter—leafy greens, fenugreek, turmeric, dandelion root, rhubarb, aloe vera, and coffee

Astringent—beans, lentils, yellow split peas, chickpeas, potatoes, cabbage, broccoli, green beans, alfalfa sprouts, tart apples, unripe banana, pomegranate, and turmeric

Spiritual Qualities of Foods

(from the teachings of Paramhansa Yogananda)

It's helpful to know not only the physical, but also the spiritual and psychological qualities of foods, and how they affect our consciousness.

Fruits	Qualities
Apples/Pears	Peacefulness
Bananas	Calmness and humility
Berries	Purity of thought
Cherries	Cheerfulness
All citrus fruits	Banish melancholy; stimulate the brain
Coconuts	Generally spiritualizing
Dates	Tenderness; sweetness
Figs	Soften a too-strict sense of discipline
Grapes	Devotion; divine love
Peaches	Selflessness; concern for others

Pineapple	Self-assurance
Strawberries	Dignity
Raspberries	Kindheartedness

Vegetables

Avocados	Good memory
Beets	Courage
Corn	Mental vitality
Lettuce	Calmness
Spinach	A simple nature
Tomatoes	Mental strength

Nuts

Almonds	Vital strength; sexual self-control
Peanuts	Elimination; general strength
Pine nuts/cashews	Harmonious development of the body
Pistachios	Brain development; memory

Other Foods

Cow milk	Enthusiasm; fresh spiritual energy
Egg yolk	Outwardly directed energy
Honey	Self-control
Rice	Mildness
Whole grains	Strength of character
Whole wheat	Steadfastness to principle

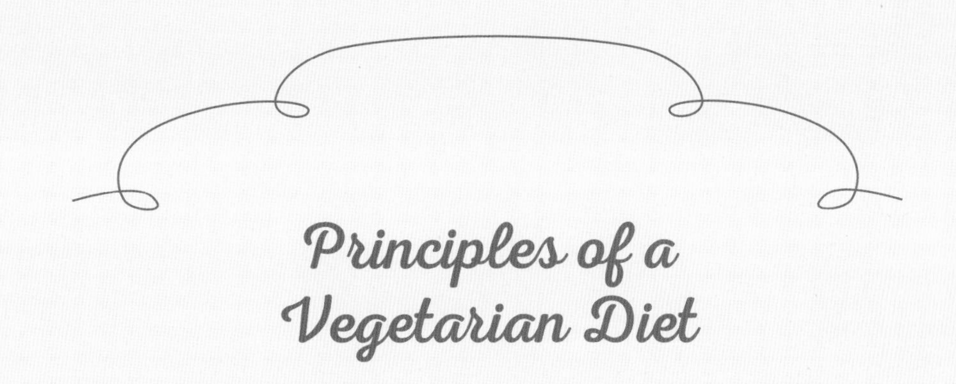

Principles of a Vegetarian Diet

> Material foods impress the mind with certain good or bad qualities; and people's thoughts, actions, and health generally are determined by the foods they eat.
>
> —*Paramhansa Yogananda*

Yogic-Vegetarian Diet

The traditional yogic diet is lacto-vegetarian, which consists of grains, legumes, fruits, vegetables, nuts, seeds, and some dairy products. A yogic diet excludes all animal flesh foods.

The yogic vegetarian diet is suggested for health, moral, and spiritual reasons, one of which is reverence for other living beings, who are also expressions of God and whose true nature is the soul. This consciousness enhances unity with all creation and expands the heart's love. (This diet expresses the principle of *ahimsa*, or non-violence.)

A yogic diet takes into account the subtle effect that food has on the mind and life force. Yogananda recommended that we choose "those material foods which emit and lodge spiritual vibrations in man's mind and brain." If we eat food with the right energy, the energy will affect our consciousness favorably.

We recommend a vegetarian diet that includes:

Whole cooked grains and legumes, cooked and some raw vegetables, and raw fruits, nuts, and seeds. Dairy products and eggs are optional.

As mentioned above, Yogananda recommended a diet of 60 percent fruits and vegetables, 20 percent protein, and 20 percent starches. This proposed ratio can be changed according to the needs of the individual. If you need more grounding, increase your protein intake, decrease fruits, and eat more vegetables that are cooked, rather than raw.

Yoga counsels eating small quantities, and choosing foods that require a minimum of energy for digestion, and that leave the body light and satisfied while providing proper nourishment and maximum life force.

If you are just beginning to explore becoming a vegetarian, you might start by eliminating beef and pork, while continuing to eat fish and chicken. Beef and pork are high in saturated fats and have been shown to be acid-forming and detrimental to good health. Instead, include in your diet more vegetarian protein, such as tofu, tempeh, beans, lentils, eggs, and dairy.

It is good to have a raw green salad at least once a day, preferably with lunch. Use a variety of salad greens. You can add raw vegetables to your salad, such as grated carrot, jicama, sprouts, cucumber, and olives.

Nature provides us with many different vegetables, grains, legumes, and other vegetarian sources for nutrition. Eating a variety of these throughout the day helps you get all the nutrients your body needs for good health. So start to experiment and have fun!

How to Plan a Menu

In part 2 of this cookbook, we offer, for each season, complete meals that are in alignment with the energetic qualities of that season. Here are some general guidelines for planning a menu:

1. Have lunch as your main meal, and a lighter meal in the evening.
2. Add variety and taste to your daily meals by combining the different vegetable groups (root, ground, leafy), different combinations of grains and beans, and different cooking techniques.
3. Create a satisfying meal by including in each meal the six tastes: sweet, salty, sour, pungent, astringent, and bitter.
4. Balance your essential nutrients by creating colorful meals, including foods that are green, red, orange or yellow, white, and brown.
5. Create a folder with your favorite recipes.
6. Plan ahead, and make a shopping list. Don't shop for food when you are hungry!

Cooking with the Seasons

Different foods have different properties, and one of the main properties is the ability to warm or cool the body. During the colder months, you will want to use warming foods, herbs, and cooking techniques. In the hotter months you'll choose foods, herbs, and cooking methods that are cooling.

During the colder months eat more warm and cooked foods, hot cereals, soups and stews, hearty grains, root vegetables, hot beverages, and heavy desserts. During the summer eat more raw foods, salads, dips, stir-fried vegetables, and cool beverages.

Additional Health Tips

- Use whole foods—mostly fresh and dried. Avoid as much as possible processed foods, or foods that have preservatives or fillers. Make your own salad dressings when possible.
- Avoid overcooking. Properly cooked foods are strengthening. Raw foods are cleansing and detoxifying.
- Fruits are best eaten alone at the beginning of a meal, or as a snack between meals.

How to Spiritualize Your Cooking

Conscious Cooking and Healthy Living

The most important aspect of preparing and cooking food is the quality of energy you put into it. That quality will be reflected in the food itself, and in how you feel after eating it. Even though each food has its own innate qualities, the consciousness and intention you put into the cooking and eating of food can help you infuse it with more spiritual upliftment.

Physical food supplies the body with energy, and good thoughts supply the mind with peace and harmony.

A positive attitude while preparing food is an important ingredient to add to your cooking. View your kitchen as a sacred space and keep it clean and orderly. You might even create a little "kitchen altar," including a photo of the loved ones for whom you are cooking.

Try to lift your consciousness before beginning to cook, and keep yourself uplifted as you cook. Think of higher consciousness flowing through you into the food. You might want to do specific things to lift your consciousness, such as beginning your cooking with a prayer, and consciously cultivating uplifting qualities such as calmness, love, gratitude, and focused attention on each part of the cooking process. Uplifting music, chanting, and the repetition of positive affirmations can help you.

You can use positive affirmations before you start cooking, while you cook, and before you eat the meal to help you stay uplifted. In this book we've included suggestions of affirmations to use during each season, to help bring balance and calmness.

Be creative in your cooking, and be patient with yourself as you change your diet. Enjoy the process.

Conscious Eating

Once you learn to eat right foods and think right thoughts, your body and mind, purified by this energy, will take on the beauty of Spirit.

—Paramhansa Yogananda

Remember: Food is a part of Spirit. We want increasingly to experience food as a channel of life force, an avenue through which God is building and maintaining the physical body. If we approach eating in the right way, it will help us draw more life force from the food.

First of all, eat only when you are hungry. Learn to distinguish between true hunger and the need to fill a void caused by emotional upset, stress, or boredom.

Create a dining area that is pleasant and uplifting. Relax a few moments after cooking the meal, so you can bring more energy to enjoying the food. Bless your food, thanking the Divine for providing it, and asking that the food may serve to build God's temple of the body.

Eat when you are calm and can concentrate on drawing energy from the food. It's good to eat in a quiet environment, undistracted by television or reading. Treat your meal with love and respect. Be conscious about enjoying the food. The more you eat with enjoyment, the more vitality you will draw from the food. Chew your food well, until it is of even consistency, before swallowing.

When you eat in such a way, you will be less likely to overeat. In any event, try to stop eating when you feel just three-quarters full. You should feel comfortable after a meal, as if you still have room in your stomach.

Then sit quietly for a few minutes to let your food begin to digest. If you eat too much or too quickly, accept yourself with good humor and understanding. See your progress as directional.

Healthy Habits of Eating

- **A simple diet is best.** Too many combinations of foods are difficult for the digestive system.
- **Avoid drinking too much with meals**, as this dilutes gastric juices and makes digestion less effective. Take fluids a half hour before or two hours after meals. But you can sip a little warm water with your meal.
- **Drink plenty of warm water or unsweetened fruit juice daily**, just not during meals.
- **Eliminate sugar**, refined starches, and fried foods, or eat them only once in a while.
- **When you want sweets or snacks**, enjoy "nature's candy": fresh fruit or unsulfured dried fruit such as figs, dates, and raisins.
- **Avoid eating late at night.** Falling asleep shortly after eating causes food to lie in the stomach without being properly digested.

- **A person with sedentary habits**, such as an office worker, should eat small quantities several times a day rather than a few large meals a day; he should fast occasionally. A person who is active or doing physical labor should eat more, and include meat substitutes, nuts, and milk.
- **Overconcentration on the palate** (appetite, cravings, and food fixations) leads to disease. It is all right to enjoy food, but you must not become a slave to it.
- **Balance your diet, then forget it.** Don't fuss about your food all the time. If you have a craving for a food that isn't good for you, don't be finicky. Eat it, but don't let this become a habit.

- **The mind is the supreme power**, and creates everything the body requires. But until you actually have that realization, you must use your common sense. It is wise to obey God's health laws, at the same time believing that the mind is the supreme force.
- **Food is important, but it's only part of our lives.** Food can help us to keep our body temple healthy and expand our consciousness. Start by introducing vegetarian foods gradually into your diet. Be relaxed and expansive about it—not rigid. Attitude is important.
- **Make sunshine, oxygen, and energy a part of your regular daily diet.** Bathe your body in the sunshine every day. Go outside daily and breathe fresh air very slowly and deeply in a relaxed way for ten to fifteen minutes, drawing in life force from the oxygen. In the winter, breathe the fresh, crisp, invigorating air.
- **Obey God's laws of hygiene and proper eating,** and keep yourself mentally filled with the strong faith that nothing can harm you, that you are ever protected.

Part 2: Essentials for Vegetarian Cooking

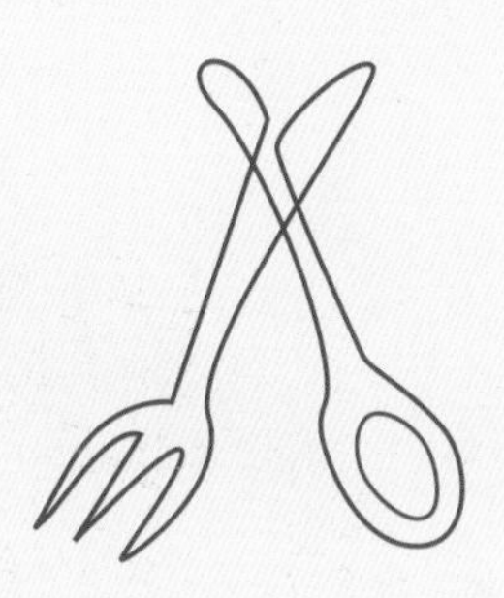

- Guidelines for Successful Cooking
- Useful Kitchen Utensils
- A Guide to Cooking Grains
- Preparing and Cooking Legumes
- Steaming Vegetables

Guidelines for Successful Cooking

Delicious meals served by a calm, happy cook are the mark of success in cooking. Knowing your ingredients and how to use them is the key to a positive outcome. Using proper kitchen equipment is also important. To achieve satisfactory results with the recipes in this book, here are some helpful guidelines. Before you know it, you'll be a confident and accomplished vegetarian cook!

- **First, choose a recipe or a menu you want to try.** Read the recipe(s) from start to finish beforehand, so that you have a clear idea of what ingredients and tools you will need.
- **Make a list of ingredients** and get them ahead of time. The recipes in this book all use foods you should be able to find in your local natural food store.
- **Give yourself time to cook.** It is best not to try new recipes when you have limited time, since they might take longer to prepare than you planned.
- **Follow the recipe as it is written.** Doing so will help you understand what was intended. The next time you use the recipe, you may make changes according to your taste.
- **You can double or halve any recipe** without adverse effects. The only change will be in the length of cooking time.
- **The number of people** to be served by each recipe is given, but this number will be affected by who is eating and what else is being served.
- **Cooking time depends on many factors.** It will vary according to your altitude, the kind of oven or stove you use, the cookware you are using, the size you cut the vegetables, the freshness of your ingredients, etc. The cooking time indicated gives an idea of how

long a specific dish can take. Use your best judgment as to whether the dish seems done, rather than relying solely on the cooking time given.

- **Preparation time** shown for each recipe refers to preliminary tasks such as chopping, blending, stirring, etc. First assemble on the counter all the food needed. Ideally, preparation should be done with focused attention, without distractions.

- **When baking,** unless otherwise specified, preheat the oven to the required temperature before putting the food into the oven.

- **Managing your time:** When making more than one dish, start with the dish that requires the longest time to prepare and cook. While waiting for ingredients to cook, steam, or marinate, use the time to prepare other ingredients or another dish. Prepare quick dishes last, so that the whole meal is ready at the same time.

- **Most of the ingredients** specified in this cookbook will be familiar to you, but a few are less common. As you follow the recipes, you will gradually familiarize yourself with the new ingredients.

- **When using tofu,** keep in mind that different brands have different consistencies. Some brands of "firm" tofu will be harder than other brands. When tofu is too firm, it will take longer to absorb the flavor of a marinade. Adjust accordingly and experiment until you find the firmness you like.

- **Use of oils:** Some of the recipes call for sautéing ingredients in oil. You can reduce the amount of oil: you just need enough to keep food from sticking to the pan. You can also begin with a water sauté, then drizzle in a very small amount of oil when the sautéing is complete.

  In this book we have specified a variety of healthy oils. Since coconut oil has been found to have so many health benefits, you can substitute coconut oil in any of the recipes. Just remember that coconut oil has its own taste, which may change the taste of the food.

- **Use of salt:** Many of the recipes use Celtic salt, which has a higher mineral content than other salt. You can, however, use sea salt or Himalayan salt instead.

- **All recipes were tested** on a conventional stove, with propane as fuel, at an elevation of 2,600 feet. At sea level foods will cook and bake faster, and at higher elevations they will take longer.

- **If a recipe calls for** an ingredient you don't have, experiment with something you have on hand, as long as it is the same type of food. For example, substitute quinoa or millet for rice, or tahini sauce for peanut butter sauce. Try substituting leafy vegetables for other leafy vegetables or root vegetables for other root vegetables. You might like the new version better than the original.

- **If a recipe calls for** an herb or spice you don't like, omit it and add something you do like. Make sure to allow for any necessary changes in cooking times and liquid quantities as a result.

- **Keep experimenting**—it will help you learn what you can and can't do in cooking. This knowledge will help you gain confidence in your own creativity, so you can have fun and enjoy cooking. I would suggest, however, that you don't experiment with new recipes when you are inviting people to dinner. It is better to make dishes you know and are confident will turn out well.

- **Don't take cooking too seriously,** for there are no absolutes. Ingredients, utensils, stoves, and ovens vary. Learning to be mentally flexible is an important step toward becoming a successful cook.

Useful Kitchen Utensils

There are a number of basic kitchen tools that will make your cooking easier and more enjoyable. You may already have some of them, so review the list below and see what you might need to add.

Basic tools

- **Cutting board**—wood or plastic. If using wood, keep it clean with water and a vegetable brush. Avoid soap since the wooden board may absorb it; be sure to dry the board completely. You can protect a wooden board from cracking by rubbing cooking oil into it occasionally. Some people prefer to have two cutting boards—one for onions, garlic, and other strong-tasting ingredients, and another for milder foods and fruits.

- **Knives**—You need three basic knives: a light vegetable knife; a small, good-quality paring knife with a sharp, pointed blade; and a serrated bread knife with a long, stainless steel blade.

- **Vegetable brush**—For cleaning vegetables and your wooden cutting board.

- **Colander**—For rinsing vegetables, and draining pasta and soaked or canned beans.

- **Fine wire-mesh strainers**—For washing grains and beans.

- **Various small utensils**—Large cooking spoon, slotted spoon, ladle, spatula, tongs, wire whisk, vegetable peeler, and kitchen scissors.

- **Measuring cups**—Most sets include the four basic sizes: ¼ cup, ⅓ cup, ½ cup, and 1 cup. Stainless steel is preferable because aluminum cups can get dented: the dent changes the size. Larger sizes are optional.

- **Measuring spoons**—A set includes the four basic sizes: ¼ tsp., ½ tsp., 1 tsp., and 1 Tbs. Stainless steel is best. If available, get also ⅓ tsp. and ½ Tbs.
- **Mixing bowls in different sizes**—Plastic and metal are both fine.
- **Blender**—For blending soups, making salad dressings and sauces, grinding nuts, and more. Works better than a food processor for creating a smooth and silky texture.
- **Food processor**—For chopping, slicing, and grating foods. Use instead of a blender when you have a large quantity of food to blend in a single batch, or when the food is of a thick consistency and difficult for a blender to process.
- **Flame "tamer" or diffuser**—A flat metal disk with holes and a handle that is placed on a gas stove burner, underneath the pan. It helps spread heat evenly and keeps food from burning or sticking to the bottom of the pan.
- **Timer**
- **Pot-holders**

Cookware

Pots, pans, and skillets—Invest in good-quality cookware, as it will last a lifetime and make a difference in the quality of your cooking. Stainless steel, cast iron, Pyrex, ceramic, or enameled cookware are the best. Aluminum is a good heat conductor, but it reacts with food, leaving traces of aluminum in it. There is some cookware on the market that uses a combination of aluminum and stainless steel, affording better heat distribution than stainless steel alone, while at the same time keeping the food from coming in contact with the aluminum.

Using a Pressure Cooker

A pressure cooker has an airtight lid that creates pressurized steam inside the cooker, which cooks the food quickly. Pressure-cooking seals in the nutrients of foods, making them more digestible and flavorful. It reduces the cooking time substantially and saves energy.

I highly recommend investing in a good stainless-steel pressure cooker and learning how to use it safely.

Learning to use a pressure cooker well involves becoming familiar with your cooker, following the safety rules and instructions on use, and learning to recognize when it gets to full pressure. Once you know how to use a pressure cooker properly, you'll be amazed at how often you'll find it useful.

Some of the recipes in this book, especially for grains and beans, call for the use of a pressure cooker.

For those who don't want to use a pressure cooker, I've included instructions in this section for how to cook without one.

Using a Rice Cooker

An electric rice cooker can also be used to cook other grains and beans, steam vegetables, and even to make soups and main and side dishes. There are some models available now that include an inner pot and a steamer to allow you to cook grains and steam vegetables at the same time. Once the rice or other food is cooked, the rice cooker automatically switches to "warm" mode, eliminating the possibility of burning the dish, and keeping the food warm without changing its taste or texture.

A Guide to Cooking Grains

The following table gives an approximate guide for amounts of water, cooking times, and yields for some of the grains. Cooking times will vary depending on the water used, the altitude where you live, and whether the grains were soaked. All information is based on using one cup of dried grain, at 2,600-foot elevation in a regular pot. Cooking at lower elevations will reduce cooking time, and cooking at a higher elevation will increase cooking time.

When increasing the amount of grain, the amount of water increases less than proportionately, because water evaporation lessens with greater amounts of grain.

Grain (1 cup dried)	Water	Cooking Time	Yield
Basmati rice (white rice)	2 cups	15 min.	3 cups
Barley (soaked overnight)	3 cups	30 min.	4 cups
Brown rice (short grain)	2½ cups	45 min.	3 cups
Brown rice (soaked overnight)	3 cups	30 min.	3½ cups
Kamut (soaked overnight)	3 cups	60 min.	3 cups
Millet	3 cups	25 min.	3½ cups
Quinoa	2 cups	15 min.	4 cups
Wild rice (soaked overnight)	3 cups	35 min.	4 cups

Remember that for those grains listed above as "soaked overnight" (barley, brown rice, kamut, and wild rice), cooking times will be longer if the grains are not presoaked.

Methods for Preparing and Cooking Legumes

Precooking preparation

Sorting and rinsing

Dry legumes need to be inspected carefully to remove any stones or shriveled and discolored beans or peas. An easy way to do that is to spread a small amount of beans, one thin layer at a time, on a tray and sort through them.

After sorting them carefully, place the beans in a bowl, add water, swirl your hand in the water, and rinse. Repeat a few times.

Soaking beans

Soaking beans is very helpful for ease of digestion, as it removes much of their indigestible sugar. In the soaking process, the beans swell as they absorb the water, so they will cook more thoroughly and in less time. The length of soaking time depends on the size and age of the beans. After soaking beans, the soaking water is not used for cooking, but is discarded.

There are two methods for soaking beans:

Slow soaking: Place beans and water (3 cups of water to every cup of beans) in a bowl and soak them for 6–8 hours, or overnight. If you soak them any longer, keep them in the refrigerator to avoid fermentation.

Quick soaking: In a pot, cover the beans with boiling water (3 cups of water to every cup of beans), or bring the beans and water to a boil. Boil for 2 minutes, turn heat off, and let stand for 1–2 hours covered. Drain, add fresh water, and cook.

Split mung beans and lentils do not require soaking before cooking.

Cooking Methods

Boiling

- After soaking the beans, drain and rinse them.
- Place the drained beans in a pot with fresh water, about 3–4 cups of water for each cup of dry beans.
- Bring to a boil and simmer until the beans are soft, approximately 1–2 hours. (See the chart on page 45.) The older the beans, the longer it will take to cook them. In order for beans to be digestible, they need to be cooked until very soft. If they are at all crunchy or chewy, they are not fully cooked.
- Keep the lid slightly open, and check periodically to see if more water is needed. The beans will not cook completely unless they are covered with water at all times during cooking. If foam forms on the surface of the water, skim it off and discard.

Pressure-cooking

- Using a pressure cooker to cook beans reduces the time by about half. The beans will be ready in 20–30 minutes (cooking and waiting time) if you have soaked the beans ahead of time.
- Use 2–3 times as much water as beans in the pressure cooker (or less, depending on the pressure cooker).
- Caution: Do not cook lentils or split peas in the pressure cooker as they can clog the pressure release valve.

Tips for cooking beans, to aid digestion and prevent gas:

Cooking beans with a strip of kombu, or with certain herbs and spices (see below), will aid digestion and add mild flavor to the beans. On the other hand, there are some seasonings that should not be added to beans while cooking, as they will toughen the skins of the uncooked beans and increase the length of cooking time.

- *Add while cooking:*

Kombu—A dark green sea vegetable sold in dried, wide strips. Used as a tenderizing agent when added to the beans from the start of cooking, it enhances their flavor and aids in their digestion. Use a 3" strip of kombu per 1 cup of dry beans. After cooking, you can cut the kombu into small pieces and allow it to blend with the rest of the ingredients according to the recipe, or discard it.

Dried herbs—Adding dried herbs—such as bay leaves, rosemary, cumin, coriander, or fennel—to cooking beans will aid digestion.

- *Do not add until after the beans are cooked:*

  Salt, tamari, sweeteners, and acidic flavorings, such as vinegar, lemon, and tomato. None of these ingredients should be added until the beans are cooked all the way through and are completely soft.

In general, one cup of dried beans yields about 2–3 cups cooked.

A Guide to Cooking Legumes

The following table gives the approximate amount of water needed, cooking times, and yields for some legumes. The yield is for drained cooked beans. Cooking times will vary depending on the freshness of the beans (fresh beans cook more quickly), the water used, and your altitude. All information is based on using one cup of dried beans, soaked overnight (8 hours) in 3 cups of water, and tested at 2,600-foot elevation in a regular pot. Cooking at a lower elevation will reduce cooking time, whereas cooking at a higher elevation will increase cooking time.

Bean *(1 cup dried, soaked overnight)*	**Water**	**Cooking Time**	**Yield**
Aduki beans	4 cups	1 hour	3 cups
Black beans	4 cups	1 hour	3 cups
Black-eyed peas	3½ cups	1 hour	2½ cups
Garbanzo beans	3 cups	1 hour	2½ cups
Great northern beans	4 cups	1 hour	3 cups
Green split peas	3½ cups	50 min.	2½ cups
Lima beans	4 cups	45 min.	3 cups
Navy beans	3 cups	1 hour	2½ cups
Pinto beans	4 cups	1 hour	3 cups

A Guide to Steaming Vegetables

Almost any vegetable can be lightly and healthfully cooked by steaming. You can also steam a variety of vegetables together.

Steaming requires a pot with a tight-fitting lid. You can use either a steamer pot (which is actually two pots, one of which has holes in the bottom and sits on top of and slightly inside the other) or a collapsible metal steamer placed in a pot. It is always better to slightly under-steam vegetables so that they don't get completely limp and lose their color and nutrients. Remember that even after you've turned off the heat, the steam will continue to cook the vegetables.

Steaming Vegetables Guidelines

The denser the vegetable, the longer it takes to steam. Root and ground vegetables take 5–30 minutes to steam, depending upon the vegetable, how old it is, and how large the pieces are (the smaller the pieces, the shorter the steaming time). Green leafy vegetables require only 3–10 minutes to steam, with tougher greens such as kale and collards taking longer than tender greens such as spinach or dandelion leaves.

Steaming vegetables in a pot, step-by-step

- Partially fill with fresh water—about 2 inches deep—the bottom of your steamer or a regular pot.
- Put the top part of the steamer, or the steamer basket in the pot, cover it, and bring the water to a boil.
- Meanwhile, wash and chop or slice the vegetables.

- Once the water is boiling, place the vegetables in the steamer basket or top pot.
- Cover the pot, reduce the heat, and allow to steam until the vegetables are tender (when a fork can pierce them).

Cooking Tips

- When steaming different vegetables together, put the root or ground vegetables in the steamer first, and later add the leafy vegetables. For example, if you are mixing carrots, broccoli, and collards, start steaming the carrots first, then add the broccoli, finishing by adding the collards. If you are steaming only leafy vegetables, start with the stems and add the leaves a little later.
- 3 cups of uncooked chopped greens yields 1 cup of cooked greens.
- Save water from steaming greens and use it as vegetable broth for cooking grains or making soups.
- Check the water level after a few minutes to make sure that all the water has not boiled off.
- To flavor plain steamed vegetables, drizzle them with extra-virgin olive oil, fresh lemon juice, or tamari before serving. See also the recipes for sauces and dressings.

Part 3: *Meals for All Seasons*

Blessing the Food

Blessing food before eating infuses it with harmonious energy.
Here are a few suggested prayer blessings before eating.

Prayer Before Eating

Heavenly Father, receive this food.
Make it holy.
Let no impurity of greed defile it.
The food comes from Thee.
It is to build Thy temple.
Spiritualize it.
Spirit to Spirit goes.
We are the petals of Thy manifestation,
But Thou art the Flower,
Its life, beauty, and loveliness.
Permeate our souls
With the fragrance of Thy presence.

(From Paramhansa Yogananda's *Whispers From Eternity*,
Crystal Clarity Publishers)

Food Blessing

Receive, Lord, in Thy light
the food we eat for it is Thine.
Infuse it with Thy love,
Thy energy, Thy life divine.

(This prayer can also be sung.
Words and music by Swami Kriyananda.)

Spring
MENUS

1

Walnut Lentil Paté
Pita Bread
Baked Herbed Vegetables
Marinated Vegetable Salad

2

Rice, Tofu, and Vegetable Medley
Spinach Dressing

3

Butternut Squash with Dill
Tofu Vegetable Noodle Soup

4

Nori Rolls
Dipping Sauce
Miso Soup
Edamame Beans

5

Asian Beet Soup
Vegetarian Spring Rolls with Dipping Sauce
White Basmati Rice

6

Spinace Barlety Salad with Mushrooms
Beet Salad with Walnuts and Orange-Ginger Dressing

7

Red Lentil Soup
Coconut Rice with Fresh Spinach
Herbed Peas

8

Sunflower Vegetable Balls
Sweet Tomato Sauce
Sautéed Carrots with Collard Greens
Zucchini Ribbons

*Easter Meal**
Oven-Roasted Potatoes with Herbs
Vegetable Frittata
Steamed Asparagus with Dressing
Mixed Green Salad with Sesame-Ginger Dressing
Pound Cake with Strawberries

***Follow the Bonus Video:** www.onlinewithananda.org/holidaymeals

The Secret of Radiant Health and Well-Being Is . . .

Breathing more consciously. With every breath, inhale vitality and courage into your mind and body; exhale stale thoughts, discouragement, and old habit patterns. Breathe in a sense of inner freedom; breathe out any lingering sense of bondage.

From *Secrets of Life* by J. Donald Walters (Swami Kriyananda).

Centering Before Cooking

- Spring is a time of fresh beginning and renewal. The weather starts to warm up and you can start introducing more fresh raw foods. It's an opportunity to bring new creative efforts into your cooking.
- Before cooking, take a few moments to center yourself.
- You can close your eyes, and fold your hands in a prayer (*pranam*) position in front of your heart.
- Take a few deep, purifying breaths. Fill yourself with vitality and renewed joy, and allow the divine energy to fill your whole being, infusing you with God's healing energy, so that the food you are cooking will be permeated with joyful and uplifting energy.

Suggested affirmations to use while cooking:

- New life, new consciousness now flood my being.
- Energy and joy flood my body cells! Joy descends to me!
- I joyfully manifest the power of God.
- God's joy flows through me.
- God's peace now floods my being.
- Within me lies the energy to accomplish all that I will to do!
- With calm faith, I open to Thy light.

1
Walnut Lentil Paté
Pita Bread
Baked Herbed Vegetables
Marinated Vegetable Salad

Walnut Lentil Paté

Serves 5–6. Makes 3½ cups.

Ingredients

1 cup walnuts, soaked and rinsed
1 cup French green lentils, rinsed
4 cups fresh water
2 bay leaves
1 tablespoon sunflower oil
3 cups fresh water
2 tablespoons extra-virgin olive oil or sunflower oil
1 cup minced onion
A pinch of Celtic salt
1 teaspoon dried oregano or 1 tablespoon fresh oregano
½ teaspoon garlic powder
1 teaspoon Dijon mustard
2 tablespoons fresh lemon juice
¼ teaspoon chili powder
1 teaspoon sea salt
¼ teaspoon black pepper
½ cup (packed) fresh parsley leaves

Instructions

Soak walnuts 4–8 hours or overnight in 3 cups water. Drain.

In a pressure cooker, place 1 cup rinsed French green lentils, 4 cups fresh water, 2 bay leaves, and 1 tablespoon sunflower oil (to prevent lentils from clogging valve). Secure lid of pressure cooker and bring to a boil on high heat. Lower heat and simmer for 8 minutes (or as needed according to pressure cooker used).

Turn heat off. Let pressure cooker cool down until it is safe to open. Drain lentils.

In a pan sauté 2 tablespoons extra-virgin olive oil or sunflower oil, 1 cup minced onion, and a pinch of Celtic salt. Add 1 teaspoon dried oregano or 1 tablespoon fresh oregano.

Sauté onion until golden brown. Set aside.

In a food processor, place soaked and drained walnuts, drained cooked lentils, sautéed onion, and ½ teaspoon garlic powder. Purée.

Add 1 teaspoon Dijon mustard, 2 tablespoons fresh lemon juice, ¼ teaspoon chili powder, 1 teaspoon sea salt, ¼ teaspoon black pepper, and ½ cup fresh parsley leaves. Keep blending until smooth.

Place lentil paté in a bowl. Adjust salt and pepper, if needed. Drizzle extra-virgin olive oil on top of dish to prevent drying.

Garnish with fresh oregano or parsley leaves.

Tip: Before cooking, sort lentils for little stones and other debris, then rinse them. If you are cooking the French lentils in a regular pot, soak them for 3–4 hours to reduce cooking time. In this recipe you can also use brown lentils instead of French lentils.

Pita Bread

Serves 5–6

Ingredient

1 package whole wheat pita bread, or gluten-free pita bread

Instructions

Heat oven to 350°. Stack 4 pita breads, wrap in foil, and place in oven for 10–12 minutes to warm.

Slice each pita bread in half, then each half in half. Cut each quarter in half again, making 8 triangles.

Place bowl of walnut lentil paté in center of platter and arrange wedges of pita bread around it.

Baked Herbed Vegetables

Serves 4

Ingredients

2 carrots, peeled, halved, and sliced into ¼-inch diagonals
1 small cauliflower, cut into flowerets (about 4 cups)
2 heads broccoli, cut into flowerets and including stems (about 4 cups)
1 teaspoon dried tarragon
½ teaspoon dried thyme
½ teaspoon garlic powder
1 teaspoon sea salt
¼ teaspoon black pepper
½ cup ghee or butter, melted
1 tablespoon Bragg's Liquid Aminos, or tamari

Instructions

Preheat oven to 375°.

Peel carrots, cut them in half, and slice into thin diagonals. Cut cauliflower into flowerets. Cut broccoli head into flowerets. Peel stems and cut into thin diagonals.

Put some water in bottom of a pressure cooker (about 1½–2 inches), then add steamer basket with half the vegetables. Secure lid of pressure cooker and bring to a boil on high heat. Lower heat and simmer for 30 seconds.

Turn heat off. Let pressure cooker cool down until it is safe to open. Repeat with remainder of vegetables. (If using regular pot, steam until vegetables are soft.)

In a small bowl mix 1 teaspoon dried tarragon, ½ teaspoon dried thyme, ½ teaspoon garlic powder, 1 teaspoon sea salt, and ¼ teaspoon black pepper. Add ½ cup melted ghee and 1 tablespoon Bragg's (or tamari).

Place steamed vegetables in a glass baking pan. Fold in herb and ghee mixture. Cover with foil and bake at 375° for about 30 minutes.

Marinated Vegetable Salad

Serves 4

Ingredients

½ cup extra-virgin olive oil
2 tablespoons fresh lemon juice
1 teaspoon Dijon mustard
1 teaspoon dried basil
1 teaspoon dried oregano
½ teaspoon dried thyme
1 teaspoon sea salt
¼ teaspoon black pepper
3 tablespoons chopped fresh parsley
3 tablespoons chopped fresh basil
1 tablespoon chopped fresh oregano (if available)
1 Japanese cucumber, cut into matchsticks
½ green pepper, cut into matchsticks
½ red pepper, cut into matchsticks
1 stalk celery, sliced in thin diagonals
½ cup Savoy cabbage, thinly sliced
½ cup red cabbage, thinly sliced
½ cup peas

Instructions

In a small bowl whisk ½ cup extra-virgin olive oil, 2 tablespoons fresh lemon juice, and 1 teaspoon Dijon mustard. Add 1 teaspoon dried basil, 1 teaspoon dried oregano, ½ teaspoon dried thyme, 1 teaspoon sea salt, ¼ teaspoon black pepper, 3 tablespoons fresh chopped parsley, 3 tablespoons fresh chopped basil, and 1 tablespoon fresh chopped oregano (if available). Mix and set aside.

In a large bowl place 1 cut Japanese cucumber, ½ cut green pepper, ½ cut red pepper, 1 stalk sliced celery, ½ cup sliced Savoy cabbage, and ½ cup sliced red cabbage. Mix together and add ½ cup peas. Mix dressing with vegetables. Cover and refrigerate for 1 hour to absorb flavors.

For Your Health: Renewal and new beginnings

Spring is a time of renewal and new beginnings. It's a perfect time to resolve to improve your diet. Early spring is a good time to start making the transition from more substantial winter dishes into lighter foods, such as fresh vegetables and salads. Choose bright, colorful, vibrant foods to uplift your energy—and your consciousness.

Rice, Tofu, and Vegetable Medley

Serves 4

Ingredients

1 package firm tofu, cut into ¼-inch cubes (12–16 ounces)
¼ cup Bragg's Liquid Aminos, or tamari
2 teaspoons dried basil
¼ cup sesame oil
1 cup white basmati rice or quinoa (or a mix), rinsed
2½ cups fresh water
2 stalks celery, cut into ¼-inch diagonal slices
1 medium carrot, peeled and cut into quarter rounds
1 cup fresh green beans, cut in 1½-inch pieces

Instructions

Place 1 package of cut tofu in a flat container or glass pan.

In a small bowl mix together ¼ cup Bragg's (or tamari), 2 teaspoons dried basil, and ¼ cup sesame oil. Pour marinade over tofu cubes, stir to make sure they are all coated, and let sit for at least 1 hour.

In a rice cooker, mix 1 cup rinsed white basmati rice, 2½ cups fresh water, 2 stalks sliced celery, 1 medium cut carrot, 1 cup cut fresh green beans, and marinated tofu cubes.

Cover rice cooker and turn it on. The cooker will turn itself off when all the water has been absorbed, and will keep it warm. Fluff with a fork and serve.

Tip: Instead of rice you can use other grains, such as quinoa. You can also vary the vegetables and herbs according to your taste.

Spinach Dressing

Makes ⅔ cup

Ingredients

¼ cup extra-virgin olive oil
1 tablespoon fresh lemon juice
2 tablespoons water
½ teaspoon garlic powder
½ teaspoon salt
¼ teaspoon black pepper
2 cups chopped fresh baby-spinach leaves

Instructions

In a blender put ¼ cup extra-virgin olive oil, 1 tablespoon fresh lemon juice, 2 tablespoons water, ½ teaspoon garlic powder, ½ teaspoon salt, ¼ teaspoon black pepper, and 2 cups fresh chopped baby spinach leaves (adding a little at a time). Blend.

Serving suggestion: For color, add to the Rice, Tofu, and Vegetable Medley plate a few slices of cucumber, some cherry tomatoes, and parsley sprigs. Serve Spinach Dressing on the side.

For Your Health: **Don't compromise**

Everyone is super-busy these days. But being short on time doesn't mean you have to eat unhealthy foods. With a little planning and creativity, you can quickly prepare healthy foods during those busy times when your body most needs good nourishment.

3 Tofu Vegetable Noodle Soup

Butternut Squash with Dill

Tofu Vegetable Noodle Soup

Serves 6–8

Ingredients

¼ cup sunflower oil
1½ cups minced onion
1 clove garlic, peeled and minced
1 carrot, peeled and cut into half rounds
2 cups bok choy, thinly sliced
2 tablespoons fresh ginger, peeled and grated
1 cup chopped green cabbage
1 cup broccoli florets, cut into small pieces
1 cup sliced white button mushrooms
6 cups water
1 package firm tofu (14–16 ounces), cut into ¼-inch cubes
4 ounces udon noodles (or buckwheat or rice noodles)*
3 tablespoons sesame oil
6 tablespoons raw tahini*
2 tablespoons mellow miso*
2 tablespoons Bragg's Liquid Aminos, or tamari
1 cup broth from soup

* See glossary.

Instructions

In a pressure cooker, heat ¼ cup sunflower oil on medium heat. Add 1½ cups minced onion and 1 clove minced garlic, and sauté until onions are golden. Add 1 cut carrot, 2 cups thinly sliced bok choy, 2 tablespoons fresh grated ginger, 1 cup chopped green cabbage, 1 cup cut broccoli florets, and 1 cup sliced white button mushrooms. Sauté for 5 minutes.

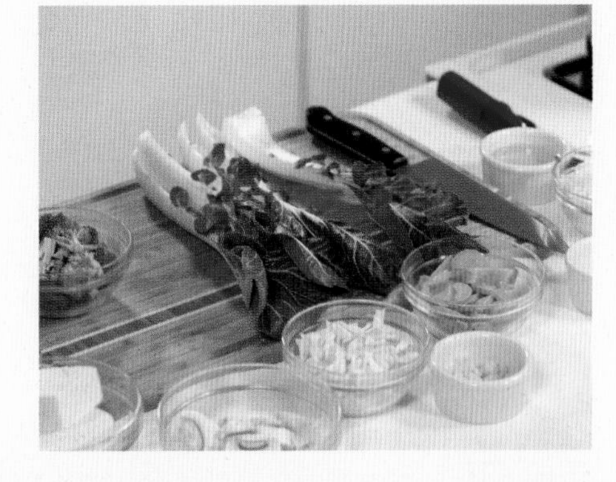

Add 6 cups water and 1 package cubed tofu. Secure lid of pressure cooker and bring to a boil on high heat. Lower heat and simmer for 5 minutes (the time required will vary for different pressure cookers). Turn heat off. Let pressure cooker cool down until it is safe to open.

While soup is cooking, break 4 ounces udon noodles into thirds. Bring a pot of water to a boil. Add noodles and simmer until cooked (about 8 minutes).

After pressure cooker can be opened, place 3 tablespoons sesame oil, 6 tablespoons raw tahini, 2 tablespoons mellow miso, 2 tablespoons Bragg's (or tamari), and 1 cup broth from soup in a blender. Blend.

Add blended miso mixture and the cooked noodles to soup before serving.

Tip: If you need to reheat soup later, make sure to warm but not boil it. If miso is boiled, it will lose its beneficial digestive enzymes.

Butternut Squash with Dill

Serves 4

Ingredients

6 cups butternut squash (1 medium squash), peeled, seeded, and cut into long strips
2 tablespoons melted ghee or butter
2 tablespoons sunflower oil
1 cup minced onion
A pinch of Celtic salt
½ teaspoon dried dill weed
¼ teaspoon black pepper
Fresh springs of dill

Instructions

Preheat oven to 375°.

Place 6 cups of cut butternut squash on baking tray and drizzle with 2 tablespoons melted ghee or butter to coat. Bake approximately 40 minutes, until the squash pieces are soft. After 40 minutes, turn oven off, and keep squash in oven for 10 minutes to finish cooking.

In a skillet warm 2 tablespoons sunflower oil on medium heat. Add 1 cup minced onions and a pinch of Celtic salt and sauté until onions are golden brown. Then add ½ teaspoon dried dill weed and ¼ teaspoon black pepper.

Mix with squash strips and garnish with fresh springs of dill. Serve warm.

Tip: To prepare butternut squash, cut in half, crosswise, and peel. Then cut each piece in half lengthwise, and scoop out the seeds. Cut the pieces of squash into 3-inch-long by ½-inch-thick strips. Butternut squash can be stored up to three months in a cool place, at 55° to 60° Fahrenheit.

***For Your Health:* Balancing food types**

When you eat vegetarian meals, make sure you have a balance between protein and starch. It's easy to overdo the starches—too much starch can make you feel sluggish or gain weight. When you make sure you have lots of vegetables and protein, your food will give you both energy and strength.

4
Nori Rolls
Dipping Sauce
Miso Soup
Edamame Beans

Nori Rolls with **Dipping Sauce**

Serves 4 rolls (24–32 pieces)

Ingredients

- 1⅓ cups short grain brown rice, soaked and drained
- 4 cups water
- 3½ cups water
- A pinch of Celtic salt
- 1 carrot, peeled and cut lengthwise into ¼-inch-thick strips
- ½ red bell pepper, cut into thin strips
- 4 cups water
- A few pinches of sea salt
- ½ Japanese cucumber, peeled and cut lengthwise into ¼-inch strips
- 3 tablespoons gold sesame seeds
- 3 tablespoons black sesame seeds (if available)
- ½ avocado, cut into strips
- 4 sheets toasted sushi nori*
- ¼ cup water
- 2–4 tablespoons Bragg's Liquid Aminos, or tamari
- 1-inch piece of fresh ginger, thinly sliced
- 1–2 teaspoons honey
- Pickled ginger
- Wasabi

* See glossary.

Instructions

Soak 1⅓ cups short grain brown rice overnight in 4 cups water. Drain.

Place soaked and drained rice in a pressure cooker with 3½ cups water and a pinch of Celtic salt. Secure lid of pressure cooker and bring to a boil on high heat. Lower heat and simmer for 10 minutes (or as needed according to pressure cooker used).

Turn heat off. Let pressure cooker cool down until it is safe to open. The rice should have absorbed all the water and be sticky. Let it sit to cool.

In a medium-size pot, bring 4 cups of water to a boil. Add a few pinches of sea salt.

When the water is boiling, add carrot strips. Simmer for 2–3 minutes to blanch the carrots. Add only small batches at a time so that the water doesn't lose its boil.

Place cold water and ice in a bowl. To test if the vegetables are tender, remove one piece with a slotted spoon, dip it into the ice water and taste. As soon as the vegetables are done, remove and submerge them in the ice water. Let the vegetables remain in the ice water until they cool. The cooling takes only a few minutes.

Repeat with strips of red bell pepper. Set aside.

In a separate bowl, place ½ cut Japanese cucumber.

In a dry skillet, toast 3 tablespoons gold sesame seeds and 3 tablespoons black sesame seeds.

Place ½ cut avocado in a bowl and set aside.

Unwrap 4 toasted nori sheets. Each sheet has a shiny and a dull side. Place 1 sheet, shiny side down, on a bamboo sushi mat or plastic wrap. Have a small bowl of cold water nearby to wet your hands and keep them from sticking to the rice.

Place 1 cup of cooked rice on the center of the nori sheet. Wet hands and pat the rice evenly, leaving a 1-inch space at the top and bottom edges of the sheet. Sprinkle 1 tablespoon of sesame seeds on rice. Arrange the cucumber, carrot, red bell pepper, and avocado strips horizontally in 2 or 3 rows, lined up with bottom line (close to you) of rice.

Using your fingers, moisten the far edge of the nori (away from you) lightly with water. Then tuck the edge close to you and roll with the bamboo mat, pressing firmly to keep a uniform shape and size. When you come to the end of the rice, allow the pressure of the roll to seal the edges. Repeat with the other 3 nori sheets.

Slice each nori roll with a sharp knife into 8 round pieces. Wipe the knife with a wet towel between cuts. Place the pieces on a platter and sprinkle with more sesame seeds.

Tips:
- 1⅓ cups of short grain brown rice make 4 cups of cooked rice. You will use 1 cup of cooked rice for each nori roll. Instead of brown rice, you can use white rice, sushi rice, or quinoa. Please adjust the amount of water used for cooking, and decide whether soaking is needed according to which grain is used.
- Keep the nori sheets in a ziplock bag, to keep them dry. Moisture makes them too soft to roll.

Variation: You can add to your nori rolls marinated, sliced tofu, blanched spinach leaves, sprouts, and/or any other vegetables you like. For these nori rolls, I use brown rice, a variety of vegetables, and avocado. You can add tofu, tempeh, or any other vegetable or grain mixture you like.

Dipping Sauce

Place ¼ cup water, 2–4 tablespoons Bragg's (or tamari), and a 1-inch piece of thinly sliced ginger in a pot. Bring to a boil and simmer on low heat for 5 minutes. Strain before serving. For a less salty flavor, add 1–2 teaspoons honey.

Miso Soup

Serves 4–5

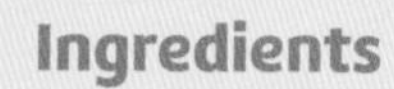

Ingredients

2 tablespoons sesame oil
1 cup minced onion
A pinch of Celtic salt
1 medium-size carrot, cut into quarter rounds
2 cups fresh shiitake mushrooms, thinly sliced
1½ tablespoons fresh ginger, peeled and grated
6 cups water
1 cup firm tofu, cut into ¼-inch cubes
4 green onions, sliced into thin rounds
10-inch wakame, broken into small pieces
2 tablespoons Bragg's Liquid Aminos, or tamari
¼ cup mellow miso*

* See glossary.

Instructions

Heat 2 tablespoons sesame oil in a pot on medium heat. Add 1 cup minced onion and a pinch of Celtic salt. Sauté until golden. Then add 1 medium-size cut carrot, 2 cups thinly sliced fresh shiitake mushrooms, and 1½ tablespoons fresh grated ginger, and sauté for another few minutes.

Add 6 cups of water, bring to a boil, and simmer for 10 minutes. Then add 1 cup cubed tofu, 4 thinly sliced green onions, and wakame pieces, and simmer for another 5 minutes.

Then add 2 tablespoons Bragg's (or tamari). If you are planning to eat all the soup in one sitting, put ¼ cup mellow miso into a mesh strainer. Use a wooden spoon or spatula to dissolve the miso into the soup by pushing it against the strainer. If you are eating only some of the soup, place 1 tablespoon of mellow miso in individual bowls. Add some broth and stir to dissolve. Then add some soup.

Note: If you need to reheat the soup later, make sure to warm but not boil it. If miso is boiled, it will lose its beneficial digestive enzymes.

Tip: Wakame, which is a seaweed, needs 5 minutes to soak in order to soften. It will expand as it hydrates. Crumble the wakame and add it at the end of cooking the soup, or soak it in cold water and add to the soup just before serving. Prolonged cooking or soaking of wakame makes it soggy and overly soft.

Variation: If you prefer not to use wakame, then, before serving, add 2 cups fresh spinach, cut into strips.

Edamame Beans

Serves 4

Ingredients

1 pound edamame beans*
(fresh or frozen)
4–6 cups water
A few pinches of Celtic salt
A few pinches of sea salt

* See glossary.

Instructions

In a pot bring 4–6 cups of water to a boil, adding a few pinches of Celtic salt. Add edamame beans, bring to a boil again, and simmer the beans for about 5 minutes.

Edamame beans should be firm yet soft. Remove pot from burner. Drain beans. If you like, sprinkle a few pinches of sea salt over the hot beans. Serve hot or cold.

For Your Health: **Explore**

It's fun to explore new kinds of healthy foods. They can even offer an introduction to another culture. And you just might discover new sources of healthy and tasty vegetarian foods. This meal is inspired by Japanese cuisine.

5 Asian Beet Soup

Vegetarian Spring Rolls with Dipping Sauce
White Basmati Rice

Asian Beet Soup

Serves 5–6

Ingredients

- 2 medium-large size beets, cut into ½-inch chunks
- Beet or chard stems, cut into thin diagonal slices
- ¼ cup sesame oil
- 2 cups chopped Napa cabbage stems
- 5 cups water
- 3 inches kombu* (seaweed), cut by hand into small pieces
- 10 inches wakame* (seaweed), cut into small pieces
- Beet or chard leaves, cut into thin slices
- Napa cabbage leaves, cut into thin slices
- ½ cup water
- 1 tablespoon arrowroot
- 2 tablespoons brown miso
- 1 teaspoon rice vinegar
- 2 tablespoons toasted sesame oil
- Sea salt to taste, if needed

* See glossary.

Instructions

Separate leaves from 2 beets. Peel and cut into ½-inch chunks.

In a pressure cooker, heat ¼ cup sesame oil on medium heat and add sliced beet stems and 2 cups chopped Napa cabbage. Sauté for a few minutes. Add 5 cups water, cut kombu, and cut beets. Secure lid of pressure cooker and bring to a boil on high heat. Lower heat and simmer for 3 minutes (the time required will vary for different pressure cookers).

Turn heat off. Let pressure cooker cool down until it is safe to open. When you can open pressure cooker, add cut wakame, sliced beet leaves, and sliced Napa cabbage leaves. Cover with lid. Let sit for 5 minutes to soften wakame and green leaves.

Meanwhile, mix ½ cup water and 1 tablespoon arrowroot in a bowl. Add 2 tablespoons brown miso and mix well. Strain mixture through a strainer for smooth consistency. Mix with soup, then add 1 teaspoon rice vinegar, 2 tablespoons toasted sesame oil, and sea salt to taste, if needed.

Tip: If you can't find beets with their leaves, use green or red chard leaves instead. Chard is a member of the beet family. The texture of chard and beet greens is similar.

Vegetable Spring Rolls
with Dipping Sauce
Serves 4 (12 spring rolls)

Ingredients

Approximately ½ cup sesame oil
8 ounces extra-firm tofu, cut into ½-inch-wide slices
Sea salt
2–3 tablespoons Bragg's Liquid Aminos, or tamari
5 green onions, chopped
3 collard leaves, stemmed and cut into thin strips
1 large carrot, peeled and cut into 3-inch-long matchsticks
3 inches of burdock, peeled and cut into 1½-inch-long matchsticks
¼ medium cabbage, thinly sliced
1 cup mung bean sprouts
¼ cup water
1 tablespoon Bragg's Liquid Aminos, or tamari
1½ teaspoons arrowroot* powder
2 teaspoons mellow miso* paste
2 teaspoons toasted sesame oil
3 tablespoons Bragg's Liquid Aminos
1 teaspoon rice vinegar
1 package square egg wraps (6 x 6 inches)

* See glossary.

Instructions

In a small skillet, heat 2 tablespoons of sesame oil on medium heat. Add the strips of tofu and a sprinkle of sea salt, and sauté until tofu is golden brown on the outside. Keep turning tofu until all sides are crisp and golden. Turn heat off and drizzle immediately with Bragg's (or tamari), allowing it to be absorbed into the tofu.

Using a second skillet or wok, warm 2 tablespoons of sesame oil on medium heat. Add chopped green onions and sauté for a few minutes. Next, add collard strips and sauté briefly. Add a bit of water to steam collards, covering skillet with a lid. Next, add and mix the cut carrot, cut burdock, and a sprinkle of sea salt. Drizzle additional sesame oil if needed. Add and mix cabbage strips and a sprinkle of sea salt. Last, add and mix mung bean sprouts. Cover and cook vegetables until soft, but crisp.

Meanwhile, in a small bowl, mix ¼ cup water, 1 tablespoon Bragg's (or tamari), 1½ teaspoons arrowroot, and 2 teaspoons mellow miso paste. Strain mixture through a strainer for smooth consistency. When vegetables are cooked, make an indentation in the center of the vegetables, add sauce, and let heat until it starts to bubble. Then fold the sauce into the vegetables. Turn heat off.

To assemble rolls, place a bowl of fresh water near the work area and transfer sautéed vegetables and tofu strips to separate bowls. Placing vegetable wrap like a diamond, spoon 2 tablespoons of vegetables at bottom end of wrap, and add slice or two of tofu on top. Fold bottom corner up to cover tofu and vegetables, then fold side corners in. Dab some water along top corner of wrap, then fold down to close and seal.

In a large skillet, heat a ⅛-inch layer of oil of sesame oil to fill skillet. Add as many vegetable wraps as you can fit in the skillet. They will take just a few minutes to turn golden. Flip each wrap over and let both sides become golden. Remove from skillet and place on a paper towel to absorb oil.

To prepare the dipping sauce, put 2 teaspoons toasted sesame oil, 3 tablespoons Bragg's, and 1 teaspoon rice vinegar in a small bowl. Mix well.

White Basmati Rice

Serves 4

Ingredients

1 cup white basmati rice, rinsed
2½ cups water
½ teaspoon Celtic salt

Instructions

In a rice cooker, place 1 cup rinsed white basmati rice, 2½ cups water, and ½ teaspoon Celtic salt. Turn rice cooker on and let cook until done.

For Your Health: **Nurturing others**

Cooking with family members is a great way to connect with them, while nurturing them with good food. Cooking with your children shows them healthy ways of cooking and eating, and it's a lot of fun.

Spinach Barley Salad with Mushrooms

Serves 4

Instructions

In a pressure cooker, place 1 cup rinsed barley, 2½ cups water, and a pinch of Celtic salt. Secure lid of pressure cooker and bring to a boil on high heat. Lower heat and simmer for 8 minutes (the time required will vary for different pressure cookers).

Turn heat off. Let pressure cooker cool down until it is safe to open.

Meanwhile, in a skillet warm 2 tablespoons sunflower oil and 2 tablespoons extra-virgin olive oil on medium heat. Add 2 tablespoons sesame seeds and 6–8 finely chopped green onions and sauté for 2 minutes. Add 2 cups sliced white button mushrooms and a pinch of Celtic salt. Cover skillet and sauté for 5 minutes. Stir in 4 cups fresh chopped spinach and cook for 2 more minutes.

Ingredients

1 cup pearled barley, rinsed (2–3 times in cold water)
2½ cups water
A pinch of Celtic salt
2 tablespoons sunflower oil
2 tablespoons extra-virgin olive oil
2 tablespoons sesame seeds
6–8 green onions, finely chopped
2 cups sliced white button mushrooms
A pinch of Celtic salt
4 cups chopped fresh spinach
2 tablespoons Bragg's Liquid Aminos, or tamari
¼ teaspoon black pepper

Combine sautéed vegetables with cooked barley, along with 2 tablespoons of Bragg's (or tamari) and ¼ teaspoon of black pepper.

Tip: If the barley didn't absorb all of the water during cooking, strain off any excess water before combining the barley with vegetables.

Beet Salad with Walnuts and Orange-Ginger Dressing

Serves 4

Ingredients

- 2 medium-size red beets, peeled and grated
- ¼ cup fresh orange juice
- 2 tablespoons fresh lemon juice
- 1 tablespoon maple syrup
- 1½ teaspoons fresh ginger root juice*
- ½ cup feta cheese, crumbled
- ½ cup toasted walnuts
- ¼–½ cup (packed) fresh cilantro leaves

* See glossary for how to make ginger juice.

Instructions

In a bowl place 2 peeled and grated red beets.

In a small bowl mix ¼ cup fresh orange juice, 2 tablespoons fresh lemon juice, 1 tablespoon maple syrup, and 1½ teaspoons fresh ginger root juice.

Mix dressing with grated beets. Add ½ cup crumbled feta cheese and ½ cup toasted walnuts. Garnish with fresh cilantro leaves.

For Your Health: Choose fresh foods

The better you eat, the better you will feel. Eating is meant to nurture and energize our bodies. Try to choose fresh foods that are filled with vitality, not foods that are overly processed. As you eat fresh foods, your body absorbs that vitality and will *want* that kind of food.

Red Lentil Soup

Serves 4

Ingredients

3 tablespoons sunflower oil
1 cup minced onion
2 celery stalks, chopped
2 cups chopped green cabbage
1 cup chopped turnip
2 medium carrots, peeled and cut into quarter rounds
1 cup red lentils, rinsed (2–3 times)
½ teaspoon garlic powder
½ teaspoon powdered cumin
1 teaspoon ground coriander
¼ teaspoon turmeric
4 cups water
2 tablespoons Bragg's Liquid Aminos, or tamari
½ teaspoon salt
¼ teaspoon black pepper
1 pinch cayenne pepper

Instructions

In a pressure cooker, warm 3 tablespoons sunflower oil on medium heat. Add 1 cup minced onion, and sauté until onions are golden (about 5 minutes).

Add 2 chopped celery stalks, 2 cups chopped green cabbage, 1 cup chopped turnip, and 2 peeled and cut carrots, and sauté for 3 more minutes.

Next, add 1 cup rinsed red lentils, ½ teaspoon garlic powder, ½ teaspoon powdered cumin, 1 teaspoon ground coriander, ¼ teaspoon turmeric, and 4 cups water. Secure lid of pressure cooker and bring to a boil on high heat. Lower heat and simmer for 5 minutes. Turn heat off. Let pressure cooker cool down until it is safe to open.

Puree soup, add 2 tablespoons Bragg's (or tamari), ½ teaspoon salt, ¼ teaspoon black pepper, and a pinch of cayenne pepper.

Coconut Rice with **Fresh Spinach**

Serves 4

Ingredients

- 1 cup white basmati rice, rinsed
- 2½ cups water
- ½ teaspoon Celtic salt
- 2 tablespoons ghee or sunflower oil
- ⅓ cup unsweetened shredded coconut
- 2 cups fresh spinach, cut into thin strips
- ½ teaspoon sea salt

Instructions

In a rice cooker, place 1 cup rinsed white basmati rice, 2½ cups water, and ½ teaspoon Celtic salt.

Cover with lid, turn rice cooker on, and cook until ready. (Most rice cookers will take about 20 minutes.) When rice is cooked, fluff with a wooden spoon.

In a skillet, warm 2 tablespoons ghee on medium heat. Add 1 cup shredded coconut and sauté until golden. Turn off heat, add and mix 2 cups fresh cut spinach and ½ teaspoon sea salt, then add the spinach-coconut mixture.

Herbed Peas

Serves 4–6 (Makes 4 cups)

Ingredients

- ¼ cup extra-virgin olive oil
- 1 cup minced onion
- ½ teaspoon garlic powder
- 2 teaspoons dried sage
- ½ teaspoon sea salt
- 2 tablespoons nutritional yeast
- ⅓ cup water
- 4 cups frozen peas, thawed (or fresh if available)
- ¼ cup minced fresh parsley leaves

Instructions In a skillet, heat ¼ cup of extra-virgin olive oil on medium heat. Add 1 cup minced onion and sauté until golden (about 5 minutes).

Mix in ½ teaspoon garlic powder, 2 teaspoons dried sage, ½ teaspoon sea salt, 2 tablespoons nutritional yeast, ⅓ cup water, and 4 cups thawed peas. Cover, reduce heat to low, and simmer for 10 minutes.

Turn heat off and sprinkle with ¼ cup fresh minced parsley leaves. Serve warm.

For Your Health:

Be creative in your cooking

When cooking, it's easy to get into a routine and repeat the same menus again and again. That's fine. The body likes routine, and it's good to keep things simple. Yet you can still be creative by making small changes to keep yourself inspired, fresh, and adventuresome.

8 Sunflower Vegetable Balls

Sweet Tomato Sauce
Sautéed Carrots with Collard Greens
Zucchini Ribbons

Sunflower Vegetable Balls

Makes 15 (1¼-inch diameter) or 30 (1-inch diameter)

Ingredients

- 1½ cups sunflower seeds or walnuts
- ¾ cup minced onion
- 1 clove garlic, peeled
- 1 stalk celery (without leaves), chopped
- 2 eggs
- 2 tablespoons minced fresh parsley
- 1 cup breadcrumbs
- 1 teaspoon sea salt

Instructions

Preheat oven to 375°.

In a food processor, grind in succession 1½ cups sunflower seeds or walnuts, ¾ cup minced onion, 1 clove peeled garlic, and 1 stalk chopped celery.

In a bowl combine 2 eggs, 2 tablespoons fresh minced parsley, 1 cup breadcrumbs, and 1 teaspoon sea salt.

Add ground ingredients to mixture in bowl. Add more breadcrumbs or nuts if needed to create a firm consistency.

Roll into balls. (1-inch diameter will make 30 balls. 1¼-inch diameter will make 15 balls. You can use an ice cream scooper to create even-sized balls.) Then flatten the balls by pressing lightly with your fingers. Put on an oiled baking sheet and bake for 45 minutes. Turn the balls after 20 minutes to cook evenly on both sides and to avoid sticking and burning.

Sweet Tomato Sauce

Makes 1¾ cups

Ingredients

- 2 tablespoons sunflower oil
- ½ cup minced onion
- A pinch of Celtic salt
- 1½ cups minced soft, ripe tomatoes
- ½ cup water
- 1 teaspoon powdered vegetable broth
- 1 tablespoon fresh lemon juice
- 1 tablespoon maple syrup
- ½ teaspoon salt, or to taste
- ⅛ teaspoon black pepper, or to taste

Instructions

In a skillet, warm 2 tablespoons sunflower oil on medium heat. Add ½ cup minced onion and a pinch of Celtic salt, and sauté until onions are golden.

Add 1½ cups minced tomatoes. Stir together so that the tomatoes are coated with onions and add ½ cup water.

Bring to a boil and add 1 teaspoon powdered vegetable broth, 1 tablespoon fresh lemon juice, and 1 tablespoon maple syrup. Turn heat down, cover, and simmer for 5 minutes. Add ½ teaspoon salt and ⅛ teaspoon black pepper (or to taste). Blend in a blender until smooth. Serve tomato sauce with nut balls.

Sautéed Carrots with **Collard Greens**

Serves 4

Ingredients

2 tablespoons sunflower oil
2 carrots, peeled and cut into thin diagonals
4 collard leaves, stemmed and cut into thin slices
2 tablespoons extra-virgin olive oil
A pinch of Celtic salt

Instructions

In a skillet, heat 2 tablespoons sunflower oil on medium heat. Add cut carrots and sauté for a few minutes.

Add and mix in 4 thinly sliced collard leaves, 2 tablespoons extra-virgin olive oil, and a pinch of Celtic salt. Cover and simmer until collard greens are soft (about 5 minutes). Add a little water if needed.

Zucchini Ribbons

Serves 4

Ingredients

3 medium-size green zucchini, shaved into long, wide strips
3 medium yellow summer squash, shaved into long, wide strips (if not available, add 3 more medium-size green zucchini)
2 tablespoons butter or extra-virgin olive oil
A sprinkle of sea salt
A sprinkle of black pepper
¼ cup minced fresh parsley
¼ cup minced fresh dill

Instructions

Place the strips of zucchini and squash in a large bowl. Divide the ribbons into 2 to 3 batches, to fit the size of the skillet used.

In a skillet, melt 2 tablespoons butter on low to medium heat.

Add one batch of ribbons and sauté until they soften (about 2–4 minutes). Add a drizzle of extra-virgin olive oil, and a sprinkle of sea salt and black pepper, and mix.

Repeat with the remaining batches.

After sautéing all batches, mix the ribbons with ¼ cup fresh minced parsley and ¼ cup fresh minced dill.

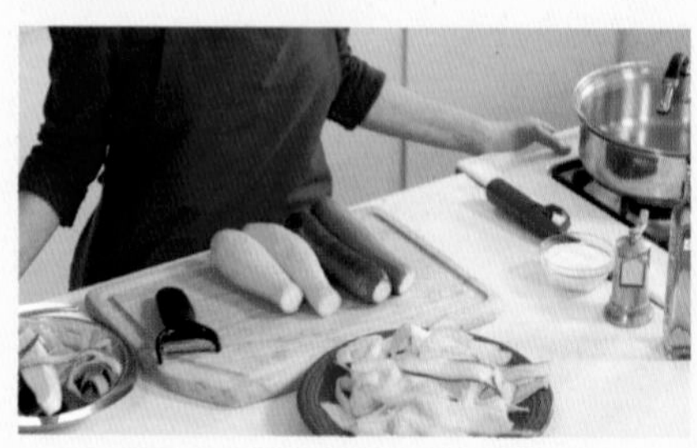

Tip: Zucchini is cooling and refreshing for the body. It is a great food for when you're feeling overheated.

Serving suggestion: Place on 3 separate platters: Zucchini Pasta; Sautéed Carrots with Collard Greens; and Sweet Tomato Sauce with Baked Nut Balls, sprinkled with minced parsley leaves.

For Your Health: Bring beauty into your cooking

Spring is a time when all of nature is full of vitality and beauty. We can bring those qualities into our cooking by creating a feast of color. Use a variety of colors to bring balance and nutrition into your meals, and have fun!

Easter Meal
Oven-Roasted Potatoes with Herbs
Vegetable Frittata
Steamed Asparagus with Dressing
Mixed Green Salad with Sesame-Ginger Dressing
Pound Cake with Strawberries
Follow the Video
*Follow the Bonus Video: www.onlinewithananda.org/holidaymeals

Easter is a time of renewal and new beginnings in all aspects of life. Offer this meal as a celebration of new possibilities for everyone at your table. Give them not only good food, but appreciation for their positive qualities. In this way you will sow seeds of greater personal fulfillment for everyone.

Easter Centering and Affirmation

Bring your awareness to the point between the eyebrows, the center of higher consciousness. Take a few purifying breaths and affirm:

"Today I will plow the garden of life with the seeds of my new creative efforts. I will sow the beginnings of wisdom, health, prosperity, and happiness, and will wait for the Divine to give me my much-needed harvest."*

* From *Meditations and Affirmations* (October–December 1942, *Inner Culture* magazine) by Paramhansa Yogananda.

Oven-Roasted Potatoes with Herbs

Serves 4

Ingredients

6 red potatoes, washed and cut into 1-inch chunks
4 tablespoons melted butter or ghee
3 tablespoons (packed) fresh rosemary leaves
1½ teaspoons dried thyme
1 teaspoon sea salt
½ teaspoon black pepper

Instructions

Preheat oven to 425°. In a large bowl toss potatoes with 4 tablespoons melted ghee. Add 1½ teaspoons dried thyme, 1 teaspoon sea salt, ½ teaspoon black pepper, and 3 tablespoons fresh rosemary leaves. Mix.

Spread potatoes on baking sheet in a single layer. Bake approximately 50 minutes or until potatoes are golden brown, crisp on the outside and soft on the inside. Turn potatoes every 15 minutes. Add sea salt to taste.

Vegetable Frittata

Serves 6

Ingredients

2 cups small broccoli florets
1 cup water
¼ cup extra-virgin olive oil
1 cup minced onion
½ cup red bell pepper, cut into ⅓-inch cubes
A pinch of Celtic salt
8 eggs
1 teaspoon sea salt
½ teaspoon black pepper
½ teaspoon paprika
⅓ cup sunflower seeds, ground
1 cup feta cheese, crumbled (4 ounces)

Instructions

Preheat oven to 350º. Boil about 1 cup water in a pot. Place broccoli florets in a steamer basket and steam until crisp but still tender (about 5–8 minutes). Set aside.

Warm ¼ cup extra-virgin olive oil in a skillet on medium heat. Add 1 cup minced onion, ½ cup cubed red bell pepper, and a pinch of Celtic salt, and sauté until soft (about 5 minutes). Set aside.

In a big bowl, beat 8 eggs. Add 1 teaspoon sea salt, ½ teaspoon black pepper, and ½ teaspoon paprika. Mix. Then, add in this order: ⅓ cup ground sunflower seeds, 1 cup crumbled feta cheese, sautéed onion mixture, and steamed broccoli. Mix.

Pour mixture into an oiled 9-inch glass pie plate. Bake for 40 minutes or until eggs are set. Remove from oven and serve warm, or let cool and serve at room temperature. Cut into wedges.

Steamed Asparagus with Dressing

Serves 4–5

Ingredients

1 pound fresh asparagus, rinsed, with end of stems removed
1 cup water
A sprinkle of sea salt
A sprinkle of black pepper
A squeeze of fresh lime juice

Instructions

Boil about 1 cup of water in a pot. Place asparagus in steamer basket and steam until crisp but still tender (4–5 minutes). Remove from steamer basket and arrange on a platter.

Before serving add a sprinkle of sea salt, a sprinkle of black pepper, and a squeeze of fresh lime juice.

Mixed Green Salad with Sesame-Ginger Dressing

Makes ⅔ cup

Ingredients

⅓ cup extra-virgin olive oil
2 tablespoons tahini paste
1½ tablespoons fresh ginger, peeled and grated
1 tablespoon chopped green onions (only the green part)
1½ teaspoons rice vinegar
1½ teaspoons Bragg's Liquid Aminos
1 teaspoon sesame oil
½ teaspoon Dijon mustard
½ teaspoon honey

Instructions

In a blender put ⅓ cup extra-virgin olive oil, 2 tablespoons tahini paste, 1½ tablespoons fresh grated ginger, 1 tablespoon chopped green onions, 1½ teaspoons rice vinegar, 1½ teaspoons Bragg's, 1 teaspoon sesame oil, ½ teaspoon Dijon mustard, and ½ teaspoon honey. Blend.

Toss dressing with mixed salad greens and any other desired salad ingredients.

Pound Cake with Strawberries

Serves 8

Ingredients

1¼ cups whole wheat pastry flour
½ cup yellow cornmeal
¼ teaspoon sea salt
½ cup agave
¾ cup unsalted butter, at room temperature, cut into small pieces
1 teaspoon vanilla extract
3 large eggs
3 cups strawberries, washed and cut into small pieces
2 tablespoons maple syrup, or to taste
Whipping cream (optional)

Instructions

Preheat oven to 325°. Butter an 8½ x 4½-inch loaf pan. Line bottom of pan with parchment paper.

In a bowl combine 1¼ cups whole wheat pastry flour, ½ cup yellow cornmeal, and ¼ teaspoon sea salt.

In a large bowl use an electric mixer to beat ½ cup agave and ¾ cup room-temperature unsalted butter (cut into small pieces), until light and fluffy. Mix in 1 teaspoon vanilla extract.

Add 3 large eggs, one at a time, beating well after each addition.

Gradually add dry ingredients, mixing just until blended. Spoon batter into prepared pan. Smooth top. Bake cake until golden brown and tester inserted into center comes out clean (about 1 hour).

Cool cake in pan on rack for 10 minutes. Turn out cake onto rack, remove parchment paper and cool for 20 minutes. (You can prepare cake 1 day ahead: cool completely, wrap tightly in plastic and store at room temperature. Before serving, re-heat cake until slightly warm.)

In a bowl combine 3 cups cut strawberries and 2 tablespoons maple syrup or to taste. Let sit for ½ hour to allow berries to release their juices and absorb sweetener.

Slice cake into ½-inch slices. Serve warm with berries and whipping cream.

Tips:

- Washing strawberries after you cut them makes them taste fresher.
- You can serve with whipping cream, coconut whipped cream (see pg. 222), or plain yogurt.

Easter is a time symbolizing
the eventual resurrection
of our little, individual selves
into the one, Infinite Self.

Swami Kriyananda

Summer

MENUS

1

Aduki Bean Salad

Carrot Cilantro Salad

Stir-Fry Zucchini with Red Bell Pepper

2

Hummus

Bulgur Salad—Tabouli

Olive Spread

Raw Cut Vegetables

Pita Bread

3

Asparagus Soup

Lima Beans with Vinaigrette

Tomato Basil Salad

4

Garbanzo Marinade with Tomatoes

Colorful Rice Salad

Tahini Eggplant with Mushrooms

5

Quinoa with Cauliflower

Raw Kale Salad

Green Almond Pesto

6

French Lentils with Cilantro

Indian Rice with Cashews

Coconut Carrot and Green Beans

7

Coconut Soup with Lemon Grass

Asian Rice Noodle Salad

8

Split Pea Soup with Ginger

Cashew Rice with Grated Beets

Sesame Spinach Salad

Fourth of July Meal*

Dill Potato Salad

Asian Sesame Coleslaw

Sunburgers • Corn on the Cob

Ice Cream or Coconut Bliss with Berries

***Follow the Bonus Video:** www.onlinewithananda.org/holidaymeals

Summer Meals

The Secret of Radiant Health and Well-Being Is . . .

Eating more fresh, raw food. Remember, your food consists of more than chemicals. Choose foods that are rich in life-force..

From *Secrets of Life* by J. Donald Walters (Swami Kriyananda).

Centering Before Cooking

- In the summer, when the weather is hot, focus on eating more fresh vegetables and fruits and using light cooking methods. While cooking, emphasize coolness and calmness. To avoid irritability and tension, focus on sharing love—and cook with the consciousness of joyful, harmonious service, without attachment to results, and without strain.
- Before cooking, take a few moments to center yourself.
- Close your eyes, and take a few deep, slow, cooling breaths. Inhale peace, exhale any tension. Inwardly relax and fill your being with inner peace. Allow your heart to soften and expand, infusing your cooking with love.

Suggested affirmations to use while cooking:

- I am calm. I am poised.
- Lord, fill me with peace and harmony.
- I radiate love and goodwill to soul friends everywhere.
- Waves of joy surge upward in my spine.
- Left and right and all around—life's harmonies are mine.
- I rise joyfully to meet each new opportunity.
- I am a wave of peace on the ocean of peace.

1

Aduki Bean Salad

Carrot Cilantro Salad
Stir-Fry Zucchini with
Red Bell Pepper

Aduki Bean Salad

Serves 5

Ingredients

1 cup aduki beans* (presoaked)
4 cups water
2 bay leaves (optional)
1 tablespoon lemon juice
2 tablespoons extra-virgin olive oil
1½ tablespoons Bragg's Liquid Aminos
1½ teaspoons cumin powder
1½ teaspoons coriander powder
2 tablespoons minced fresh parsley
1 cup fresh green beans, trimmed and halved
¼ cup sunflower seeds

* See glossary.

Instructions

Place rinsed and presoaked aduki beans in a pressure cooker with 4 cups water and 2 bay leaves (optional). Secure lid of pressure cooker and bring to a boil on high heat. Lower heat and simmer for 5 minutes (or as needed according to pressure cooker used).

Turn heat off. Let pressure cooker cool down until it is safe to open.

For dressing, mix in a bowl 1 tablespoon lemon juice, 2 tablespoons extra-virgin olive oil, 1½ tablespoons Bragg's, 1½ teaspoons cumin powder, 1½ teaspoons coriander powder, and 2 tablespoons fresh minced parsley. Set aside.

Place 1 cup trimmed and halved green beans in a steamer basket over boiling water. Steam until crisp but still tender (about 5 minutes).

Place ¼ cup sunflower seeds in a dry skillet over medium heat. (High heat will burn seeds.) Lightly toast, stirring often. Set aside.

When aduki beans are done, drain and mix with dressing and steamed green beans. Just before serving, mix the toasted sunflower seeds with the aduki bean salad.

Carrot Cilantro Salad

Serves 3–4

Ingredients

- 2 cups carrot, peeled and grated (about 4 medium-size carrots)
- 2 tablespoons extra-virgin olive oil (optional)
- 2 tablespoons fresh lemon juice
- 1 tablespoon fresh ginger root juice*
- 2 teaspoons maple syrup
- ¼ cup minced fresh cilantro leaves

* See glossary for how to make ginger juice.

Instructions

Mix in a bowl 2 tablespoons extra-virgin olive oil, 2 tablespoons fresh lemon juice, 1 tablespoon fresh ginger root juice,* 2 teaspoons maple syrup, and ¼ cup fresh minced cilantro leaves. Add in 2 cups peeled and grated carrots. Mix well. Let sit to absorb flavors (about 10 minutes). Serve.

Tip: Most of the nutrients of carrots are concentrated under the skin. If you are using organic carrots, try not to peel off the skin. To clean the carrots, simply use a hard brush to scrape them.

Stir-Fry Zucchini with Red Bell Pepper

Serves 4

Ingredients

- 2 tablespoons butter, or sunflower oil
- ½ red bell pepper, cut in half lengthwise, then cut into thin strips
- 2 green zucchini, halved lengthwise, cut into ¼-inch rounds
- 2 yellow crookneck squash, halved lengthwise, then cut into ¼-inch rounds
- 2 tablespoons Bragg's Liquid Aminos
- A pinch of freshly ground black pepper

Instructions

Warm 2 tablespoons butter or oil in a wok on medium heat. Add red bell pepper strips and sauté for 2–3 minutes.

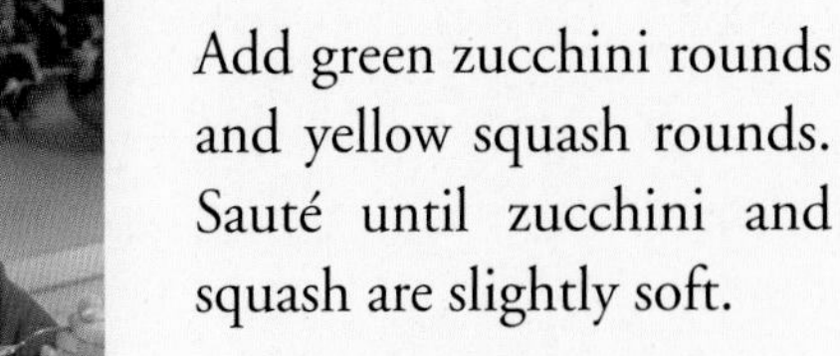

Add green zucchini rounds and yellow squash rounds. Sauté until zucchini and squash are slightly soft.

Add 2 tablespoons Bragg's and pinch of black pepper. Serve warm or cold.

2

Hummus

Bulgur Salad—Tabouli
Olive Spread
Raw Cut Vegetables
Pita Bread

Hummus

Serves 5

Ingredients

- ¾ cup of garbanzo beans (also called chickpeas), presoaked
- 4 cups fresh water
- 3 tablespoons tahini (roasted)
- 1 teaspoon sea salt
- 2 tablespoons extra-virgin olive oil
- 2 tablespoons fresh lemon juice
- 2 cloves garlic, peeled and minced (optional)
- 2 tablespoons (packed) fresh parsley leaves
- 1 pinch cayenne
- 2 pinches paprika

Instructions

Place soaked, rinsed garbanzo beans in pressure cooker and add 4 cups water to cover. Secure lid of pressure cooker and bring to a boil on high heat.

Lower heat and simmer for about 10 minutes (the time required will vary for different pressure cookers). Turn heat off. Let pressure cooker cool down until it is safe to open.

Blend in food processor until smooth, 2 cups cooked garbanzo beans, ⅔ cup water (can use water from cooking beans), 3 tablespoons tahini, 1 teaspoon sea salt, 2 tablespoons extra-virgin olive oil, and 2 tablespoons fresh lemon juice. If desired, add 2 cloves minced garlic. Add 2 tablespoons parsley leaves, a pinch of cayenne, and 2 pinches paprika. Blend for 1 minute.

Bulgur Salad—Tabouli

Serves 5–6

Ingredients

- 1 cup cracked bulgur wheat,* rinsed
- 1⅓ cups boiling water
- 1 medium tomato, diced
- 1 cucumber, peeled and diced
- 2 green onions, minced (green and white parts)
- 1 cup minced fresh parsley leaves
- ¼ cup minced fresh mint
- ¼ cup extra-virgin olive oil
- 2 tablespoons fresh lemon juice
- 1½ teaspoons sea salt, or to taste

* See glossary.

Instructions

In a bowl place 1 cup rinsed bulgur wheat and 1⅓ cups boiling water.

Cover and let sit for 45 minutes. Fluff with a fork.

In another bowl mix 1 medium diced tomato, 1 diced cucumber, 2 minced green onions, 1 cup fresh minced parsley leaves, ¼ cup minced fresh mint, ¼ cup extra-virgin olive oil, 2 tablespoons fresh lemon juice, and 1½ teaspoons sea salt.

Combine bulgur with marinade, and let sit for about 20 minutes to absorb flavors. Serve at room temperature.

Tip: You can substitute refined bulgur for the cracked bulgur wheat. You will need to add 1 cup water to 1 cup bulgur. Bulgur is made of wheat berries. If you are allergic to wheat, you can make this dish with other light grains, such as cooked quinoa or white basmati rice.

Olive Spread

Makes 2 cups

Ingredients

3 cups sliced black olives (canned)
1 tablespoon dried oregano
1 large garlic clove, peeled and minced
⅓ cup extra-virgin olive oil

Instructions

In a food processor place 3 cups sliced black olives, 1 tablespoon dried oregano, 1 large clove minced garlic, and ⅓ cup extra-virgin olive oil.

Blend using a pulse method so it has a coarse texture. Be careful not to overblend.

Tip: If you are buying canned olives, choose those with low sodium content.

Raw Cut Vegetables

Serves 6–8

Ingredients

3 stalks celery, cut in 3-inch pieces
3 carrots, quartered lengthwise and cut in 3-inch pieces
½ green bell pepper, cut in thin slices
½ yellow bell pepper, cut in thin slices
½ red bell pepper, cut in thin slices
½ jicama, cut in pinky-finger-sized pieces

Instructions

The vegetables can be cut ahead of time and kept fresh in water in the refrigerator. When ready to serve, pat vegetables dry with a towel and arrange on a platter.

Pita Bread

Serves 5–6 (4 pita breads)

Ingredients 1 package store-bought pita bread (whole wheat, white, or gluten-free)

Instructions Heat oven to 350°. Stack pita bread, wrap in foil, and place in oven for 10–12 minutes. Slice each pita bread in half, then each half in half. Cut each quarter in half again, making 8 triangles.

Serving Suggestion: Place hummus in a bowl and sprinkle extra-virgin olive oil on top to prevent drying. Decorate with paprika, sprigs of parsley or mint, and whole or sliced olives. Place bulgur salad on top of lettuce leaves. Serve meal with a jar of water with lemon and orange slices and fresh mint, to keep cool.

For Your Health: Harmonize ingredients and cooking styles with the seasons

One of the secrets of healthy eating is to harmonize ingredients and cooking styles with the season. In the summer, try to use more raw vegetables, salads, dips, and lightly cooked foods. These foods help to cool and refresh your body, give you a feeling of lightness, and allow your body to adjust better to the heat.

3
Asparagus Soup
Tomato Basil Salad
Lima Beans with Vinaigrette

Asparagus Soup

Serves 4–5

Ingredients

¼ cup extra-virgin olive oil
2 leeks, minced (white part only)—
about 2 cups
A pinch of Celtic salt
½ teaspoon garlic powder
1 teaspoon dried dill
1 pound fresh asparagus
5 cups water
2 tablespoons vegetable broth powder
½ cup rolled oats
1½ teaspoons sea salt, or to taste
¼ teaspoon black pepper, or to taste

Instructions

Wash 1 pound fresh asparagus. Cut the woody stringy stem ends from each spear and discard. Cut into 1-inch pieces.

In a 4-quart pot, warm ¼ cup extra-virgin olive oil on low heat. Add 2 cups minced leek and a pinch of Celtic salt. Sauté for 4 minutes.

Mix in ½ teaspoon garlic powder, 1 teaspoon dried dill, and cut asparagus. Add 5 cups water, 2 tablespoons vegetable broth powder, and ½ cup rolled oats.

Bring to a boil and simmer for about 12 minutes. Let cool. Puree soup in a blender or food processor, or with an immersion blender, until smooth. Add 1½ teaspoons sea salt and ¼ teaspoon black pepper, or to taste.

Serving Suggestion: This soup can be served chilled in warm weather.

Variation: Instead of dried dill, use 1 tablespoon minced fresh dill. If using fresh dill, add it after the soup is cooked and before it is blended.

Tomato Basil Salad

Serves 4

Ingredients

2 large ripe tomatoes, washed and cut
into about 10 wedges each
1 tablespoon extra-virgin olive oil
½ teaspoon dried basil
½ teaspoon sea salt
A pinch of black pepper

Instructions

In a bowl mix 1 tablespoon extra-virgin olive oil, ½ teaspoon dried basil, ½ teaspoon sea salt, and a pinch of black pepper.

Fold in tomato wedges. Let marinate for 15–30 minutes before serving.

Serving Suggestion: Place lima beans with vinaigrette on a bed of lettuce. Add tomato basil near the lima beans. Ladle soup and add a sprig of dill.

Lima Beans with Vinaigrette

Serves 4

Ingredients

1 cup lima beans, presoaked (with 2 bay leaves, or a 3-inch piece of kombu*)
4 cups water
¼ cup extra-virgin olive oil
2 tablespoons fresh lemon juice
2 tablespoons minced fresh Italian parsley leaves
½ teaspoon dried basil
½ teaspoon oregano
½ teaspoon marjoram
1 teaspoon sea salt
¼ teaspoon black pepper
6–8 lettuce leaves

* See glossary.

Instructions

Place presoaked beans in pressure cooker and add 4 cups water and 2 bay leaves (optional). Secure lid of pressure cooker and bring to a boil on high heat. Lower heat and simmer for 4 minutes (the time required will vary for different pressure cookers).

Turn heat off. Let pressure cooker cool down until it is safe to open.

In a glass jar place ¼ cup extra-virgin olive oil, 2 tablespoons fresh lemon juice, 2 tablespoons fresh minced parsley leaves, ½ teaspoon dried basil, ½ teaspoon oregano, ½ teaspoon marjoram, 1 teaspoon sea salt, and ¼ teaspoon black pepper. Shake well.

Add dressing to beans, lightly mix, and serve at room temperature on a bed of lettuce leaves.

Variation: Soak ⅓ cup of sun-dried tomatoes in boiling water for 15 minutes, to soften. Then mince and add to salad.

For Your Health: Keep your eating environment pleasant and uplifting

The environment in which we eat has an impact on our state of consciousness. Try to make your eating environment pleasant and uplifting. The food will nurture you more if you don't read a book, watch TV, or talk on the phone while you eat. Just focus on enjoying the food and absorbing its nutrients.

4
Garbanzo Marinade with Tomatoes
Colorful Rice Salad
Tahini Eggplant with Mushrooms

Garbanzo Marinade with Tomatoes

Serves 4

Ingredients

1 cup garbanzo beans, presoaked
4 cups water
2 bay leaves
2 tablespoons sesame seeds
1 cup minced tomatoes
¼ cup extra-virgin olive oil
¼ cup Bragg's Liquid Aminos
¼ teaspoon black pepper
¼ cup minced fresh parsley
2 tablespoons sesame seeds, toasted

Instructions

Place presoaked garbanzo beans, 4 cups water, and 2 bay leaves in a pressure cooker. Secure lid of pressure cooker and bring to a boil on high heat. Lower heat and simmer for 8 minutes (the time required will vary for different pressure cookers).

Turn heat off. Let pressure cooker cool down until it is safe to open.

In a dry skillet, toast 2 tablespoons sesame seeds until light brown. Set aside.

In a bowl mix 1 cup minced tomatoes, ¼ cup extra-virgin olive oil, ¼ cup Bragg's, and ¼ teaspoon black pepper. Let sit to marinade for 15–20 minutes.

In a separate bowl, mix 1 cup cooked garbanzo beans with ¼ cup fresh minced parsley and 2 tablespoons toasted sesame seeds. Let sit for 5 minutes to absorb flavors. Add marinade.

Colorful Rice Salad

Serves 6

Ingredients

3 cups water
1½ cups white basmati rice, rinsed
½ teaspoon Celtic salt
¼ cup extra-virgin olive oil
6 green onions, minced
½ red bell pepper, cut in ¼-inch cubes
½ yellow bell pepper, cut in ¼-inch cubes
¼ cup pine nuts
Sea salt and black pepper to taste
¼ cup minced fresh parsley
¼ cup minced fresh dill

Instructions

In a rice cooker, place 3 cups water, 1½ cups rinsed white basmati rice, and ½ teaspoon Celtic salt. Turn rice cooker on and let cook. Set aside rice cooker.

In a saucepan warm ¼ cup extra-virgin olive oil on low–medium heat. Add 6 minced green onions, ½ red bell pepper (cubed), and ½ yellow bell pepper (cubed). Sauté for 3–5 minutes. Add ¼ cup pine nuts and sauté for a few more minutes.

Mix sautéed vegetables with cooked rice. Add sea salt and black pepper to taste. Garnish with ¼ cup minced fresh parsley and ¼ cup minced fresh dill.

Tip: Instead of a rice cooker, you can use a regular pot. Bring to boil 4 cups water, add 2 cups rinsed white basmati rice and ½ teaspoon Celtic salt. Simmer until all the water is absorbed and the rice is cooked (approximately 10–15 minutes). While rice is simmering, partially cover pot with lid.

Tahini Eggplant with Mushrooms

Serves 3–4

Ingredients

3 small Japanese eggplants, cut into 1-inch cubes (about 3 cups)
2 tablespoons extra-virgin olive oil
2 cups sliced white button mushroom (cut off the stems)
2 tablespoons extra-virgin olive oil
3 tablespoons raw tahini
⅓ cup water
2 tablespoons fresh lemon juice
1 teaspoon dried dill weed
1 teaspoon powdered cumin
1 teaspoon sea salt
¼ teaspoon black pepper
1 pinch cayenne pepper
¼ cup minced fresh parsley

Instructions

Place 3 cups of cubed eggplant in a steamer and steam until soft (8–10 minutes).

In a skillet warm 2 tablespoons extra-virgin olive oil on low–medium heat. Add 2 cups sliced mushrooms and sauté for 5 minutes. Add 2 more tablespoons extra-virgin olive oil and steamed eggplant cubes. Sauté for a few more minutes. Set aside.

In a blender put 3 tablespoons raw tahini, ⅓ cup water, 2 tablespoons fresh lemon juice, 1 teaspoon dried dill weed, 1 teaspoon powdered cumin, 1 teaspoon sea salt, ¼ teaspoon black pepper, and a pinch of cayenne pepper. Blend well.

In a bowl place sautéed eggplant and mushrooms. Fold in tahini dressing. If needed, add salt and pepper to taste. Garnish with ¼ cup minced fresh parsley.

For Your Health: **Uplifting company**

When eating, we are especially open to outside influences. When you are enjoying a meal with friends, keep the conversation uplifting.

5 Quinoa with Cauliflower

Raw Kale Salad
Green Almond Pesto

Quinoa with **Cauliflower**

Serves 5

Ingredients

2¼ cups water (or vegetable stock)
2 tablespoons vegetable broth
1 tablespoon sunflower oil
1 cup quinoa,* rinsed
2 cups cauliflower, washed and chopped into small florets
2 carrots, grated (about 1 cup)
½ cup chopped fresh parsley

* See glossary.

Instructions

Add 2 tablespoons vegetable broth and 1 tablespoon sunflower oil to 2¼ cups water. Bring to boil and stir in 1 cup rinsed quinoa. Reduce heat to simmer. Cover partially and simmer until water is absorbed (15–20 minutes).

Cover fully and let sit 5 minutes. Fluff with a fork.

While quinoa is cooking, steam 2 cups chopped cauliflower until soft (about 10 minutes). Meanwhile, mix together in a bowl 1 cup grated carrots and ½ cup chopped parsley. When quinoa is done, mix with parsley and grated carrots. Gently mix in cauliflower.

Raw Kale Salad

Serves 6

Ingredients

¼ cup extra-virgin olive oil
2 tablespoons fresh lemon juice
2 tablespoons Bragg's Liquid Aminos, or tamari
1 tablespoon sesame seeds
1 large bunch fresh green or Russian kale, washed, dried, stemmed, and cut into thin strips

Instructions

In a bowl mix ¼ cup extra-virgin olive oil, 2 tablespoons fresh lemon juice, 2 tablespoons Bragg's (or tamari), and 1 tablespoon sesame seeds. Add stemmed and cut kale.

Cover and refrigerate for at least 1 hour before serving.

Tip: You can cut Russian kale into thin strips. Because green kale is curly, just cut into small pieces. When kale is fresh, it has a sweet and slightly bitter-pungent flavor. When it's old, its bitter tone increases. You can substitute kale for cabbage whenever you want a bright green color and additional chlorophyll.

Raw Dijon Kale Salad (Alternative Recipe)

Serves 4–6

Ingredients

1 teaspoon Dijon mustard
¼ cup nutritional yeast
⅓ cup extra-virgin olive oil
2 tablespoons lemon juice
1 teaspoon Bragg's Liquid Aminos
1 large bunch fresh green kale, washed, dried, stemmed, and cut into small pieces

Instructions

In a bowl mix 1 teaspoon Dijon mustard, ¼ cup nutritional yeast, ⅓ cup extra-virgin olive oil, 2 tablespoons lemon juice, and 1 teaspoon Bragg's. Add stemmed and cut kale.

Cover and refrigerate for at least 1 hour before serving.

Green Almond Pesto

Makes 1 cup

Ingredients

½ cup almonds, soaked and peeled (or cashews or walnuts)
2 cups (packed) basil leaves (or 1 cup cilantro and 1 cup parsley)
¾ cup extra-virgin olive oil
2 tablespoons water
1 tablespoon fresh lemon juice
½ teaspoon sea salt
1–2 cloves garlic, minced (optional)

Instructions

Soak ½ cup almonds (or cashews or walnuts) overnight, peeling the next morning.

Place ½ cup soaked, peeled almonds in blender and grind until almonds are finely ground. Add ¾ cup extra-virgin olive oil and 2 tablespoons water, 2 cups (packed) basil leaves, 2 tablespoons fresh lemon juice, ½ teaspoon sea salt, and 1–2 cloves minced garlic (if desired). Blend until smooth.

Tip: For thinner consistency, add more oil as desired.

For Your Health: **Balanced diet**

Maintain a balanced diet. Never overeat. Make it a practice to leave the table feeling that you could have eaten more.

French Lentils with Cilantro

Serves 3–4

Ingredients

1 cup French lentils, rinsed
4 cups water
2–3 bay leaves
1 tablespoon sunflower oil
2 tablespoons extra-virgin olive oil
1 tablespoon Bragg's Liquid Aminos
¼ cup minced fresh cilantro

Instructions

In a pressure cooker, place 1 cup rinsed French green lentils, 4 cups fresh water, 2 bay leaves, and 1 tablespoon sunflower oil (to prevent lentils from clogging valve). Secure lid of pressure cooker and bring to a boil on high heat. Lower heat and simmer for 6 minutes (the time required will vary for different pressure cookers).

Turn heat off. Let pressure cooker cool down until it is safe to open. Drain and place lentils in a bowl. Mix lentils with 2 tablespoons extra-virgin olive oil, 1 tablespoon Bragg's, and ¼ cup fresh minced cilantro.

Tip: Before cooking lentils, sort them for little stones and other debris, then rinse them. If you are cooking the French lentils in a regular pot, soak them for 3–4 hours to reduce cooking time.

Indian Rice with Cashews

Serves 2–3

Ingredients

1½ cups water
A pinch of Celtic salt
½ cup white basmati rice, rinsed (2 cups cooked)
½ cup chopped raw cashews
2 tablespoons ghee
¼ cup black raisins
6 fresh curry leaves (if available)
½ teaspoon turmeric
2 tablespoons lime juice
½ teaspoon sea salt

Instructions

In a small pot boil 1½ cups water and a pinch of Celtic salt. Add ½ cup rinsed white basmati rice. Bring to a boil again and simmer until all water is absorbed (about 15 minutes). Set aside.

In a pan, dry roast ½ cup chopped raw cashews. Add 2 tablespoons ghee, ¼ cup black raisins, and 6 fresh curry leaves (if available). Sauté for a few minutes. Finally, add ½ teaspoon turmeric, 2 cups cooked basmati rice, 2 tablespoons lime juice, and ½ teaspoon sea salt. Serve warm.

Coconut Carrot and Green Beans

Serves 3–4

Ingredients

2 tablespoons coconut oil
1 teaspoon mustard seeds
1 cup red minced onion
1 teaspoon turmeric
1 cup carrot, ¼-inch pieces
1 cup green beans, ¼-inch pieces
A pinch of Celtic salt
½ cup water
1 teaspoon cumin powder
1–2 cloves garlic, minced
1 teaspoon sea salt
1 cup unsweetened shredded coconut

Instructions

In a larger pan, heat 2 tablespoons coconut oil and 1 teaspoon mustard seeds (allow to pop). Add 1 cup minced red onion and sauté for 3–4 minutes.

Next add 1 teaspoon turmeric, 1 cup chopped carrot, 1 cup chopped green beans, a pinch of Celtic salt, and ½ cup water. Cover and simmer for 5 minutes to soften vegetables.

Add 1 teaspoon cumin powder, 1–2 cloves minced garlic, 1 teaspoon sea salt, and 1 cup unsweetened coconut flakes. Mix well. Turn heat off and let sit for a few minutes to absorb flavors.

For Your Health: Conscious relaxation

Before you eat, consciously relax your body, mind, and especially your heart. Sit down and take a few smooth, deep breaths. Release all tension and bring yourself into the present moment. Now you'll be much more able to enjoy and absorb the flavors and nutrients in your food.

7 Coconut Soup with Lemon Grass

Asian Rice Noodle Salad

Coconut Soup with **Lemon Grass**

Serves 4–5

Ingredients

1 cup dried shiitake mushroom slices, soaked
7 ounces (½ of a 14-ounce package) firm tofu, rinsed and cut into ½-inch cubes
3 tablespoons ghee
2 stalks fresh lemon grass, trimmed and crushed (or 2 teaspoons dried)
2 tablespoons coconut oil
1 cup minced onion
A pinch of Celtic salt
2 cloves garlic, minced
2 tablespoons peeled and grated ginger root
½ teaspoon cumin powder
½ teaspoon coriander powder
⅛ teaspoon cayenne (use ¼ teaspoon for spicier flavor)
3 cups water
1 14-ounce can unsweetened coconut milk
2 tablespoons vegetable broth powder
¾ cup carrots (approximately 1½ carrots), cut into quarter rounds
2 cups Napa cabbage, thinly sliced
¼ cup minced fresh cilantro leaves

Instructions

Six hours prior to cooking, soak the dried shiitake mushrooms in water.

Rinse firm tofu and pat it dry to prevent sticking while sautéing in pan. Cut into ½-inch cubes. In a small skillet, heat 3 tablespoons ghee on medium heat. Add cubed tofu pieces and sauté until golden (about 5 minutes). Set aside.

Trim ends and tops (including any dried, brown parts) of the stalks of fresh lemon grass. Take out outer tough parts. Crush stalks and set aside.

In a pot, heat 2 tablespoons coconut oil on medium heat. Add 1 cup minced onion and a pinch of Celtic salt and sauté until translucent.

Add 2 cloves minced garlic, 2 tablespoons grated ginger, ½ teaspoon cumin powder, ½ teaspoon coriander powder, and ⅛ teaspoon cayenne. Mix. Add sautéed tofu, 3 cups water, one 14-ounce can of unsweetened coconut milk, 2 tablespoons vegetable broth powder, ¾ cup cut carrots, 1 cup soaked shiitake mushroom slices, and 2 stalks crushed lemon grass.

Bring to a boil and simmer for about 10 minutes. Add 2 cups sliced Napa cabbage and simmer for another 5 minutes.

Before serving, discard lemon grass stems, and add ¼ cup fresh minced cilantro leaves.

Tip: If using fresh lemon grass, select stalks that don't look dry or brittle. To store lemon grass, wrap the stems in a paper bag and place in the fridge for 2–3 weeks. The stems can also be frozen for several months, in a sealed plastic bag.

Asian Rice Noodle Salad

Serves 6

Ingredients

- 1 celery stalk, cut into ¼-inch diagonal slices
- ½ cup Napa cabbage, very thinly sliced
- ½ cup carrot, peeled and shaved
- ½ cup red bell pepper, cut in julienne strips
- ½ cup snow peas, strings removed
- ½ cup bean sprouts, rinsed
- A pinch of Celtic salt
- 1 tablespoon sunflower oil
- 1 package of rice noodles (14 ounces)
- 1 clove garlic
- 1½ inches fresh ginger root, peeled
- ¼ cup honey
- ¼ cup red wine vinegar
- ¼ cup Bragg's Liquid Aminos
- ¼ cup sesame oil
- ½ cup sunflower oil
- ½ cup sesame seeds, toasted
- ¼ cup fresh cilantro leaves, coarsely chopped

Instructions

Cut 1 celery stalk into ¼-inch diagonal slices; thinly slice ½ cup Napa cabbage; peel and shave ½ cup carrots; cut ½ cup red bell pepper into julienne strips; remove strings from ½ cup snow peas; and rinse ½ cup bean sprouts. Set aside.

In a pot boil 8 cups water, then add a pinch of Celtic salt and 1 tablespoon sunflower oil. Add 1 package (14 oz.) of rice noodles. Turn heat off, cover pot, and let sit for 8 minutes. Drain noodles.

In a blender put 1 clove garlic and 1½ inches of fresh, peeled ginger root, and pulse until fine. Add ¼ cup honey, ¼ cup red wine vinegar, and ¼ cup Bragg's. Blend well.

Add ¼ cup sesame oil and ½ cup sunflower oil in a slow stream with machine running to emulsify. This will make about 1½ cups dressing.

In a bowl mix rice noodles with some dressing. Add prepared vegetables (sliced celery, sliced Napa cabbage, shaved carrot, julienned red bell pepper, snow peas, and rinsed bean sprouts). Mix.

Add more dressing as desired and mix well. Garnish with ½ cup toasted sesame seeds and ¼ cup coarsely chopped fresh cilantro leaves.

For Your Health: **Adapt to your environment**

Each culture has its own cuisine wisdom. It's good to draw inspiration from other cultures and adapt their cuisines to fit your own tastes, the climate, the season of the year, and the produce that is available to you locally. This is a wonderful way to add creativity to your diet while harmonizing it with your environment.

8
Split Pea Soup with Ginger
Cashew Rice with Grated Beets
Sesame Spinach Salad

Split Pea Soup with **Ginger**

Serves 4–5

Ingredients

1 cup green split peas, rinsed
3 cups fresh water
2 tablespoons extra-virgin olive oil
1 cup minced onion
A pinch of Celtic salt
¼ cup fresh ginger root, peeled and grated
2 tablespoons vegetable broth powder
5 cups fresh water
½ cup rolled oats
2 teaspoons sea salt
Fresh parsley sprigs

Instructions

Soak 1 cup rinsed green split peas overnight in 3 cups fresh water. Drain.

In a pressure cooker, warm 2 tablespoons extra-virgin olive oil on medium heat. Add 1 cup minced onion and a pinch of Celtic salt. Sauté until translucent. Add ¼ cup peeled and grated ginger root, 2 tablespoons vegetable broth powder, 5 cups fresh water, drained peas, and ½ cup rolled oats.

Secure lid of pressure cooker and bring to a boil on high heat. Lower heat and simmer for 10 minutes (the time required will vary for different pressure cookers).

Turn heat off. Let pressure cooker cool down until it is safe to open, then remove lid and add 2 teaspoons sea salt.

Puree soup in a blender, a food processor, or with an immersion blender until smooth. Blending the soup will add a smooth, silky texture. Garnish with fresh parsley sprigs.

Cashew Rice with **Grated Beets**

Serves 2–3

Ingredients

1½ cups water
A pinch of Celtic salt
½ cup white basmati rice, rinsed (2 cups cooked)
½ cup chopped raw cashews
2 tablespoons ghee
¼ cup black raisins
6 fresh curry leaves (if available)
½ teaspoon turmeric
2 tablespoons fresh lime juice
½ teaspoon sea salt
1 cup grated raw beet (1 medium-size beet)

Instructions

In a small pot boil 1½ cups water and a pinch of Celtic salt. Add ½ cup rinsed white basmati rice. Bring to a boil again and simmer until all water is absorbed (about 15 minutes). Set aside.

In a pan, dry roast ½ cup chopped raw cashews. Add 2 tablespoons ghee, ¼ cup black raisins, and 6 fresh curry leaves (if available). Sauté for several minutes.

Add ½ teaspoon turmeric, 2 cups cooked rice, 2 tablespoons fresh lime juice, ½ teaspoon sea salt, and 1 cup grated beet.

Sesame Spinach Salad

Serves 4–6

Ingredients

- 10 ounces fresh baby spinach, washed and dried
- 1 medium carrot, grated
- 2 tablespoons sesame oil
- 2 tablespoons extra-virgin olive oil
- ⅓ cup fresh orange juice
- 2 teaspoons honey
- 1½ tablespoons fresh ginger, peeled and grated
- ½ teaspoon sea salt
- 1 pinch black pepper
- ¼ cup toasted sesame seeds

Instructions

In a bowl place 10 ounces washed baby spinach and 1 medium grated carrot. Set aside.

In a blender put 2 tablespoons sesame oil, 2 tablespoons extra-virgin olive oil, ⅓ cup fresh orange juice, 2 teaspoons honey, 1½ tablespoons ginger (peeled and grated), ½ teaspoon sea salt, and a pinch of black pepper. Blend (makes ⅔ cup dressing).

Mix dressing with spinach and carrot mix, and add ¼ cup toasted sesame seeds.

For Your Health:

Include vibrant colors and textures

Try to bring joy and creativity into your cooking. Make it fun. Choose dishes that offer vibrant colors and a variety of textures. Your cooking will become a source of inspiration, joy, and renewal.

May your kitchen be filled with friends and love ...

Fourth of July Meal
Dill Potato Salad
Corn on the Cob
Asian Sesame Coleslaw
Sunburgers
Ice Cream or Coconut Bliss with Berries
*Follow the Bonus Video: www.onlinewithananda.org/holidaymeals
Follow the Video

America's Independence Day

celebrates the nation's freedom from foreign rule. We can also celebrate *personal* freedom: freedom from past habits, mistakes, and self-limiting ways of thinking—freedom to claim our highest potential as children of God.

Fourth of July Centering and Affirmation

Try to prepare your Fourth of July meal with a sense of inner freedom, and a joyful determination to be an expression of your own highest Self. You can affirm while cooking:

"Nothing on earth can hold me!
My soul, like a weightless balloon,
soars upward through skies
of eternal freedom!"*

* From *Affirmations for Self-Healing* by Swami Kriyananda

Dill Potato Salad

Serves 4

Ingredients

6 medium red potatoes (or 12 small Yukon Gold potatoes), cut into 1-inch chunks
2 eggs, hard-boiled and chopped
1 tablespoon apple cider vinegar
½ teaspoon garlic powder
½ teaspoon salt
1 stalk celery, minced
⅓ teaspoon dry mustard
2 tablespoons extra-virgin olive oil
¼ cup mayonnaise
1 tablespoon fresh dill leaves (or 1 teaspoon dried dill)
Sea salt to taste
Paprika for garish (optional)

Instructions

In a pressure cooker, place 6 cut red potatoes and enough water to cover them. Secure lid of pressure cooker and bring to a boil on high heat. Lower heat and simmer for 3 minutes (the time required will vary for different pressure cookers).

Turn heat off. Let pressure cooker cool down until it is safe to open.

Meanwhile, in a pan place 2 eggs and enough water to cover them. Bring to a boil, lower heat to simmer, and cook for 10 minutes. Drain hot water and cover with cold water. Let sit for a few minutes to cool. Then peel and chop.

When potatoes are ready, strain them and place in a large bowl. While they are still warm, add 1 tablespoon apple cider vinegar, ½ teaspoon garlic powder, ½ teaspoon sea salt, 1 stalk minced celery, and ⅓ teaspoon dry mustard. Mix well.

When potato salad has cooled, add 2 tablespoons extra-virgin olive oil, ¼ cup mayonnaise, and 2 chopped hard-boiled eggs. Mix well. Sprinkle 1 tablespoon fresh dill leaves over potatoes. Add salt to taste. Garnish with paprika (optional).

Variations: If vegan, use ½ cup toasted sunflower seeds instead of eggs. If you enjoy dill, add ¼–½ cup extra fresh dill leaves to potato salad.

Corn on the Cob

Serves 4

Ingredients 4 ears of fresh corn, husked and trimmed

Instructions Remove the husk and all of the silks from the ears of corn.

If using pressure cooker: Place about 2 inches of water in a pressure cooker. Insert steamer basket with halves of corn. (Make sure water does not touch bottom of steamer basket.) Secure lid of pressure cooker and bring to a boil on high heat. Lower heat and simmer for 3 minutes (the time required will vary for different pressure cookers).

Turn heat off. Let pressure cooker cool down until it is safe to open. Remove hot corn with tongs.

If using regular pot: Place about 2 inches of water in pot. Add steamer basket with corn. (Make sure the water does not touch the bottom of the steamer basket.) Cover pot with lid. Bring to a boil and simmer until corn is soft, but crisp (about 15 to 20 minutes). Serve steamed corn with ghee or butter, and salt

Asian Sesame Coleslaw

Serves 4

Instructions

In a bowl mix 2 cups sliced green cabbage, 2 cups sliced red cabbage, and 1 cup grated carrot.

In a blender place 4 tablespoons apple cider vinegar, 4 tablespoons water, 4 tablespoons extra-virgin olive oil, 4 tablespoons cashews or sunflower seeds, 2 tablespoons sesame seeds, 1 tablespoon toasted sesame oil, 1 tablespoon agave nectar or honey, ½ teaspoon garlic powder, ½ teaspoon salt, and a pinch of cayenne. Blend until smooth and creamy.

Pour dressing on cabbage mixture and toss. Add salt to taste, if needed. Cover and refrigerate. Let flavors absorb for 30 minutes. Garnish with ¼–½ cup fresh chopped cilantro.

Ingredients

2 cups green cabbage, thinly sliced
2 cups red cabbage, thinly sliced
1 cup grated carrot
4 tablespoons apple cider vinegar
4 tablespoons water
4 tablespoons extra-virgin olive oil
4 tablespoons cashews or sunflower seeds
2 tablespoons sesame seeds
1 tablespoon toasted sesame oil
1 tablespoon agave or honey
½ teaspoon garlic powder
½ teaspoon salt
1 pinch cayenne
¼–½ cup chopped fresh cilantro

Sunburgers*

Makes 6 burgers

Ingredients

1½ cups ground sunflower seeds
½ cup grated carrot
½ cup celery, finely chopped
⅓ cup minced onion
1 teaspoon garlic powder
1 teaspoon dried basil
2 tablespoons minced fresh parsley
2 tablespoons Bragg's Liquid Aminos, or tamari
2 eggs
2 tablespoons sunflower oil or melted butter

Instructions

Preheat oven to 375°. Cover a baking sheet with parchment paper and brush with oil.

In a bowl mix together 1½ cups ground sunflower seeds, ½ cup grated carrots, ½ cup finely chopped celery, ⅓ cup minced onion, 1 teaspoon garlic powder, 1 teaspoon dried basil, 2 tablespoons fresh minced parsley, 2 tablespoons Bragg's (or tamari), 2 eggs, and 2 tablespoons sunflower oil.

Using a Mason jar ring (3½-inch diameter), scoop some of the mixture with a spoon and press firmly into the ring to create a patty. Distribute patties about ½ inch apart on oiled baking tray. (If you do not have a Mason jar ring, shape patties by scooping mixture with a big spoon onto the oiled tray.)

Bake for 20 minutes on one side and 10–15 minutes on the other. Both sides should be a medium brown color.

Serve with whole wheat buns. If using frozen buns, wrap them in foil and heat in oven (at 350°) for 10–15 minutes. Add your favorite condiments.

Tip: To learn how to make whole wheat buns, watch our Yeasted Bread Cooking Show online.

Variation: Instead of eggs, you can substitute a mixture of 2 tablespoons ground flax seeds and 4 tablespoons fresh water to create the consistency of an egg mixture.

Ice Cream or Coconut Bliss with Berries

Serves 4

Ingredients

1 pint vanilla ice cream or nondairy vanilla Coconut Bliss
1 cup fresh blueberries
1 cup fresh raspberries

Instructions

Serve ice cream in bowls topped with fresh berries.

* Inspired by the *Simply Vegetarian* cookbook by Nancy Mair, Crystal Clarity Publishers.

Fall

MENUS

1

Tofu Spinach Pie

Cilantro Beets

Steamed Green Beans

2

Kitchari

3

Black Beans with Yam

Kale with Sunflower Seeds

Tahini-Dill Dressing

4

Potato-Pea Curry

Marinated Beets

Tofu Savory Sauce

5

Carrot-Ginger Soup

Tofu with Collard Greens

6

Herbed Quinoa

Glazed Carrots and Parsnips

Steamed Baby Bok Choy

Tahini-Dill Dressing

7

Baked Acorn Squash

Navy Beans with Curried Fennel

Broccoli with Ginger Dressing

8

Brown Rice with Oat Groats

Sautéed Rutabaga, Turnip, and Chard

Peanut Dressing

Thanksgiving Meal*

Ananda Nut Loaf

Mashed Potatoes

Coconut Cranberry Sauce

Baked Yams • Cashew Gravy

Green Beans with Vinaigrette

Pumpkin Pie

(Gluten-, Sugar-, and Dairy-Free)

Christmas Meal*

Baked Acorn Squash with Wild Rice Mix Stuffing

Braised Broccoli with Orange Dressing

Tofu Spinach Pasties

Mushroom Gravy

Maple Walnut Pie

***Follow the Bonus Video:** www.onlinewithananda.org/holidaymeals

Fall Meals

The Secret of Radiant Health and Well-Being Is . . .

Concentrating on the vital essence of what you eat. The more you make it a practice to eat consciously, the more the energy in what you eat will fill your being—and the more, as a result, you will *want* to eat correctly.

From *Secrets of Radiant Health and Well-Being* by J. Donald Walters (Swami Kriyananda)

Centering Before Cooking

- In fall the weather becomes cold, windy, and changeable. It's time to keep the body warm and nurtured, as well as grounded, with nourishing warm meals.
- Before cooking, take a few moments to center yourself.
- Start by taking a few slow, deep, warm breaths. Consciously relax away from all your duties and responsibilities into your inner haven of peace. Don't allow the busyness of life to overwhelm you. Make an effort to cook with focused awareness, blessing the food along the way, so that it will bless and nourish those who eat it.

Suggested affirmations to use while cooking:

- I relax from outer involvement into my inner haven of peace.
- I am safe. I am sound. All good things come to me; they give me peace.
- At the center of life's storms, I stand serene.
- Strength and courage fill my body cells.
- I open to the flow of God's life within me.
- I am well! I am strong! I am a flowing river of boundless power and energy.
- Thy power within me is infinite.

Tofu Spinach Pie

Serves 4–6

Ingredients

- 1½ cups whole wheat pastry flour or filo dough
- ½ teaspoon sea salt
- ⅓ cup sunflower oil
- ¼ cup cold water
- 1 pound firm tofu
- 2 tablespoons extra-virgin olive oil
- 2 tablespoons fresh lemon juice
- 1 teaspoon garlic powder
- 2 teaspoons sea salt
- ½ teaspoon black pepper
- 2 tablespoons sunflower oil
- 1 cup minced onion
- 3 cups fresh spinach, cut into bite-sized pieces

Making the crust

Mix 1½ cups flour and ½ teaspoon sea salt in a bowl. Combine thoroughly with ⅓ cup sunflower oil.

Add ¼ cup cold water. Mix all ingredients together to create a dough. If the dough feels a bit dry, add a little more water so that all the ingredients stick together well.

Place dough in an oiled 9-inch glass pie dish. Press out evenly with fingers, starting from the center until it fully covers the bottom and sides of the dish. Prick bottom of dough with fork to prevent bubbling.

Bake for 15 minutes at 375°. Remove from oven and set aside.

Instructions

Crumble 1 pound firm tofu by hand into a bowl and mash with a fork. Add 2 tablespoons extra-virgin olive oil, 2 tablespoons fresh lemon juice, 1 teaspoon garlic powder, 2 teaspoons sea salt, and ½ teaspoon black pepper. Mix well and set aside.

Pour 2 tablespoons sunflower oil into a skillet and place on medium heat. When oil has heated, add 1 cup minced onion. Sauté until onions are golden.

Add 3 cups cut spinach and sauté for about 2 minutes or until spinach is wilted. (Do not overcook spinach as it will become watery.) Add cooked spinach and onions to tofu mixture. Spoon into baked pie crust and press down firmly with spoon so the top is uniform. Bake uncovered for 30–45 minutes at 375° until the top is firm and golden. Allow pie to sit for 5 minutes. Cut into wedges and serve.

Variation: For a creative alternative to whole wheat crust, use filo dough (available frozen in most markets). Follow directions on package. Spread half of filo sheets and cover with filling, then cover with remaining filo sheets. Alternatively, a ready-made pastry crust can be used.

Cilantro Beets

Serves 4–6

Ingredients

- 4 medium beets (optional: 2 red and 2 gold beets make for a colorful dish)
- 1½ tablespoons extra-virgin olive oil
- 1½ tablespoons fresh lemon juice
- 1 packed tablespoon whole, fresh cilantro leaves without stems

Instructions

Place 4 whole beets in a pressure cooker and add water to cover. Secure lid and turn to high heat. When pressure cooker comes to full steam, lower heat and simmer for 10 minutes (the time required will vary for different pressure cookers). Turn heat off. Let pressure cooker cool down until it is safe to open. Remove lid and allow beets to cool slightly, then peel and cut into cubes or slices. (After cooking, the skin becomes soft and is easy to peel off with the fingers.) Place beets into glass bowl.

Making the dressing

In a small bowl whisk together 1½ tablespoons extra-virgin olive oil, 1½ tablespoons fresh lemon juice, and 1 tablespoon cilantro leaves. Pour over beets. Serve warm or cold.

Steamed Green Beans

Wash fresh green beans (one handful per person) and trim ends. Place in a steamer basket over boiling water. Steam about 10 minutes or until crisp but still tender.

2 *Kitchari*

A delicious Indian stew of rice, red lentils, vegetables, and spices. Nourishing and satisfying, kitchari is easy to digest and assimilate—a complete meal in itself.

Kitchari

Serves 6–8

Instructions

Spoon 2 tablespoons ghee into pressure cooker. (Alternatively, butter may be used.)

Place pressure cooker on medium heat. When ghee has melted and heated, add 3½ teaspoons mustard seeds and 2 teaspoons cumin seeds. Both mustard and cumin seeds are warming herbs and stimulate digestion. Heating these seeds in oil releases their aromatic flavor.

As they are sautéed, the mustard seeds will begin to "pop." Add 1¼ teaspoons turmeric and 2½ tablespoons freshly grated ginger.

Ingredients

- 3½ teaspoons mustard seeds
- 2 teaspoons cumin seeds
- 1¼ teaspoons turmeric
- 2½ tablespoons fresh ginger peeled and grated
- ½ cup minced onion
- ½ cup minced celery
- ½ cup minced green cabbage
- ½ cup carrots, peeled and cut into half rounds
- 1½ cups white basmati rice, rinsed
- ½ cup butternut squash, peeled and cut into ½-inch cubes
- ½ cup green beans, fresh or frozen, cut into 1½-inch lengths
- ¾ cup red lentils, rinsed
- 6 cups water or vegetable broth
- 2 teaspoons Bragg's Liquid Aminos
- 1 teaspoon sea salt
- Black pepper to taste
- ⅓ cup (packed) fresh cilantro leaves, washed

When the ingredients are well-combined and simmering, lower the heat and add ½ cup minced onion, ½ cup minced celery, and ½ cup minced green cabbage. Continue sautéing for about 5 minutes.

Add ½ cup cut carrots, ½ cup cubed butternut squash, ½ cup cut green beans, ¾ cup red lentils, 1½ cups white basmati rice, and 6 cups water (or vegetable broth).

Secure lid of pressure cooker and turn to high heat. When pressure cooker comes to full steam, lower heat and simmer for 6 minutes (the time required will vary for different pressure cookers).

Turn heat off. Let pressure cooker cool until it is safe to open. Add 2 teaspoons Bragg's, 1 teaspoon sea salt, and black pepper to taste. Serve, garnishing with fresh cilantro leaves.

For Your Health: **Positive thinking, right attitude**

Start your cooking by adopting the right frame of mind. Get centered and positive, and try to infuse all that you do with right attitude. It's important to eat healthy foods, but positive attitude is as necessary for good health as a healthy diet.

Black Beans with **Yam**

Serves 3–4

Ingredients

1 cup black beans (presoaked)
3 cups water
2 bay leaves
2 tablespoons coconut oil
1 leek, finely chopped or minced (use white and green parts)
A few pinches of Celtic salt
2 cups yam, peeled and cut into ½-inch cubes
Bragg's Liquid Aminos (or tamari), to taste
¼ cup water

Instructions

Begin by cooking black beans. Drain the soaking water and place 1 cup black beans in a pressure cooker. Add 3 cups water and 2 bay leaves. Secure lid and turn to high heat. When pressure cooker comes to full steam, lower heat and simmer for 8 minutes (the time required will vary for different pressure cookers). Turn heat off. Let pressure cooker cool down until it is safe to open. Set aside. Keep covered until serving.

Heat 2 tablespoons coconut oil in a 10- or 12-inch cast-iron skillet. When oil is melted and heated, add 1 chopped leek and a few pinches of Celtic salt. Lightly sauté.

When the leek becomes translucent, add 2 cups cubed yam, a drizzle of Bragg's (or tamari), and ¼ cup water. Cover and simmer for about 5 minutes, or until the yam cubes are soft when pierced with a fork. Turn heat off and keep covered until serving.

Kale with **Sunflower Seeds**

Serves 3–4

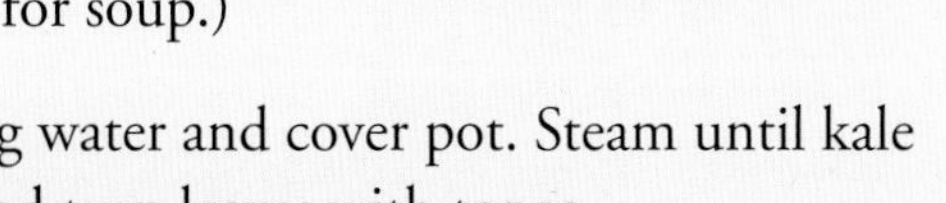

Ingredients

1 bunch of kale
½ cup toasted sunflower seeds

Instructions

Put a few inches of water in a steamer pot and put on to boil. Wash kale leaves. Cut or tear into bite-sized pieces. (You may wish to save the stems for making stock for soup.)

Place cut kale into a steamer basket, and place over boiling water and cover pot. Steam until kale is tender (about 10 minutes). Check every few minutes and turn leaves with tongs.

Turn heat off. When serving, sprinkle toasted sunflower seeds as garnish.

Tahini-Dill Dressing

Makes 1¾ cups

Place into a blender and blend until smooth:

¾ cup water
¼ cup extra-virgin olive oil
¼ cup fresh-squeezed lemon juice
½ cup tahini (roasted)
1 tablespoon maple syrup, or a pinch of stevia powder
2 tablespoons Bragg's Liquid Aminos, or tamari
½ teaspoon garlic powder
½ teaspoon dried dill or 1½ teaspoons fresh dill
¼ teaspoon sea salt
1 pinch black pepper

Serving Suggestion:
Place in middle of plate: steamed kale w/toasted sunflower seeds. At the center of the kale place black beans, leek and yam. On the side put a bowl of tahini dressing.

For Your Health:
Variety of colors and textures

One of the secrets of a balanced, healthy vegetarian diet is to include different colors. Different colors are an indication that your meal includes carbohydrates, protein, and vegetables, and a variety of minerals and vitamins. It's not only a feast for the eyes, but also good for the body. You can spread the different colors throughout the day, or include them, if possible, in one meal. Using a variety of textures in your meal will also make it more interesting and appealing.

Potato-Pea Curry

Serves 5–6

Ingredients

6 medium-size Yukon Gold potatoes
2 teaspoons Celtic salt
1½ cups peas, fresh or frozen
3 tablespoons ghee
3 tablespoons extra-virgin olive oil
1 tablespoon curry powder
1 teaspoon sea salt
2 tablespoons minced cilantro

Instructions

Wash 6 potatoes. Place whole, unpeeled potatoes in a pressure cooker and add water to cover. Add 1 teaspoon Celtic salt. (Piercing each potato with a paring knife will make it easier to peel, after cooking.)

Secure lid and turn to high heat. When pressure cooker comes to full steam, lower heat and simmer for 7 minutes (the time required will vary for different pressure cookers). Turn heat off. Let pressure cooker cool down until it is safe to open. Drain water from potatoes and peel. Place in a large bowl. Mash with a fork. Set aside.

In another pot, put 4 cups water and 1 teaspoon Celtic salt on to boil. When water begins to boil, add 1½ cups peas and simmer for 10 minutes. Drain peas and set aside.

Heat a skillet and melt 3 tablespoons ghee and 3 tablespoons extra-virgin olive oil. Stir in 1 tablespoon curry powder and turn heat off.

Add ghee mixture to mashed potatoes. Stir, adding 1 teaspoon sea salt or to taste. Gently fold in cooked peas. Add 2 tablespoons cilantro. Serve, adding more cilantro as garnish.

Marinated Beets

Serves 4–6

Ingredients

4 medium-size beets
2 tablespoons ghee
Juice of ½ lemon
Sea salt to taste

Instructions

Bake, steam, or boil 4 beets. Peel, slice into bite-sized pieces, and place in a glass bowl. Heat a small skillet and add 2 tablespoons ghee. When melted, pour ghee over beets, squeeze over them the juice of half of a lemon, and add sea salt to taste. Cover until served.

Tofu Savory Sauce*

Makes 2 cups

Ingredients

¾ cup extra-virgin olive oil
¾ cup water
¼ cup Bragg's Liquid Aminos
1½ teaspoons tamari
1½ teaspoons lemon juice
2 tablespoons nutritional yeast
¼ teaspoon kelp powder
¼ teaspoon basil
⅛ teaspoon granulated garlic powder
1 pound firm tofu

Place all ingredients, except tofu, in a blender or food processor and blend. To this mixture, add and blend: 1 pound firm tofu, rinsed well, cut in chunks. Serve this sauce warm or cold.

Serving Suggestion: A tasty complement to this meal is a green salad with cucumber, tomato slices, and toasted sunflower seeds.

For Your Health: Silence

We digest our food better when we eat in silence, without distractions. If you are eating alone, try to eat in silence, focusing on and enjoying the food you have prepared. If you are eating with others, you may suggest beginning the meal with a few minutes of silence, to allow everyone to enjoy and appreciate the flavors, before engaging in conversation. Silence helps you eat more consciously and harmoniously.

* Inspired by *Recipes from the Heart Cookbook* by The Pampered Chef.

Carrot-Ginger Soup

Serves 4–5

Ingredients

1 cup minced onion
2 stalks celery, chopped
1–2 cloves garlic, minced
1 tablespoon peeled and grated ginger (more if desired)
3 cups carrots, peeled and chopped
2 tablespoons vegetable broth powder
5 cups water
1½ teaspoons sea salt
1 tablespoon fresh lemon juice
Fresh dill for garnish

Instructions

In a pot or pressure cooker, sauté 1 cup minced onion, 2 stalks chopped celery, 1 to 2 cloves minced garlic, and 1 tablespoon peeled and grated ginger.

Add 3 cups chopped carrots, 2 tablespoons vegetable broth powder, and 5 cups water. If using a pressure cooker, secure the lid and turn to high heat. When pressure cooker comes to full steam, lower heat and simmer for 7 minutes (the time required will vary for different pressure cookers).

Turn heat off. Let pressure cooker cool down until it is safe to open.

If using a regular pot, bring to a boil and simmer for 20 minutes, or until the carrots are soft.

Allow soup to cool slightly. Dish soup in batches into a blender, or use a hand blender and blend in the pot. While blending the soup, add 1½ teaspoons sea salt and 1 tablespoon fresh lemon juice. Serve, garnishing with fresh dill.

Tofu with Collard Greens

Serves 4

Ingredients

2 tablespoons sesame oil
1 pound extra-firm tofu, cut into ½-inch cubes
Collard green leaves, cut into thin strips
Stems of 4 collard greens, chopped
1 teaspoon dried thyme
1½ tablespoons nutritional yeast
2–3 tablespoons Bragg's Liquid Aminos
¼ cup water

Instructions

Heat 2 tablespoons sesame oil in a cast-iron or regular skillet. Add 1 pound cubed tofu and sauté lightly.

Add 4 chopped collard stems, 1 teaspoon thyme, and 1½ tablespoons nutritional yeast. Drizzle 2 to 3 tablespoons Bragg's over mixture and gently turn.

Add 4 cut collard leaves and ¼ cup water. Cover and let collards cook 5 minutes or until tender.

Serving Suggestion: Serve this meal with whole wheat tortillas.

To heat tortillas in the oven, preheat oven to 250°. Wrap a stack of tortillas in aluminum foil and place on a baking sheet. If tortillas are dry, spray with a little water before warming. Place in oven for about 20 minutes.

To heat tortillas on a stove, place tortillas in a single layer in a stainless steel or cast-iron skillet over low heat. Warm for about 1 to 2 minutes on each side.

Keep tortillas warm by covering them with a slightly dampened dishtowel. For crispy tortillas, melt a little butter or ghee in a pan, then add the tortillas.

For Your Health: Flavoring foods

When you cook, flavor the food: We digest food better when we enjoy its taste! But avoid making the food excessively stimulating. The quality of the food and the taste can influence your state of consciousness. Next time you cook, be more conscious of the flavors you are adding, so that all the flavors blend together harmoniously.

Herbed Quinoa

Serves 4

Ingredients

- 2¼ cups water
- 1 cup quinoa, rinsed
- 1 teaspoon dried thyme
- 1 teaspoon dried dill weed
- ½ teaspoon ginger powder
- ¼ teaspoon garlic powder
- ¼ teaspoon sea salt
- 1 tablespoon ghee, or sunflower oil
- ¼ cup toasted slivered almonds

Instructions

Oil the insert bowl of an electric rice cooker.

Place all of the ingredients, except slivered almonds, into the rice cooker bowl. Mix well.

Cover with lid, turn rice cooker on, and cook until ready. (Most rice cookers will take about 20 minutes.)

When cooked, fluff with a wooden spoon. Let sit for a few minutes, covered, before serving. Garnish with ¼ cup toasted slivered almonds.

Variation: Use white basmati rice instead of quinoa, or a combination of both.

Glazed Carrots and **Parsnips**

Serves 4

Ingredients

2 teaspoons sunflower oil
2 teaspoons sesame oil
2 medium-size carrots, peeled and cut into sticks (pinky-finger size)
2 medium-size parsnips, peeled and cut into sticks (pinky-finger size)
A few pinches of Celtic salt
1 teaspoon dried tarragon
Bragg's Liquid Aminos
¼ cup water
¼ cup fresh parsley, washed and finely chopped

Instructions

Place skillet on medium heat. Add 2 teaspoons sunflower oil and 2 teaspoons sesame oil.

When oils heat, add 2 cut carrots and 2 cut parsnips. Put in a few pinches of Celtic salt.

Cover and simmer on low heat, checking often. Cook until a fork inserts easily into the softened vegetables.

Add 1 teaspoon dried tarragon, a drizzle of Bragg's, and ¼ cup water. Cover and keep warm until ready to serve. Garnish with ¼ cup chopped parsley.

Steamed Baby Bok Choy

Serves 4

Wash baby bok choy (1 per person) and discard any brown or wilted leaves. Place into a steamer basket and set basket over boiling water. Cover. Steam for 5 to 8 minutes, turning once with tongs halfway through. Keep warm until serving.

Tahini-Dill Dressing

Makes 1¾ cups

Place into a blender and blend until smooth:

¾ cup water
¼ cup extra-virgin olive oil
¼ cup fresh-squeezed lemon juice
½ cup tahini (roasted)
1 tablespoon maple syrup, or a pinch of stevia powder
2 tablespoons Bragg's Liquid Aminos, or tamari
½ teaspoon garlic powder
½ teaspoon dried dill, or 1½ teaspoons fresh dill
¼ teaspoon sea salt
1 pinch black pepper

***For Your Health:* Bless the food**

When the food is ready, try to relax for a few moments before eating. Then bless the food, not as a mere ritual but with conscious appreciation and gratitude. If you are sharing the meal with others, you might start by saying grace together to create a harmonious atmosphere and a high vibration.

Baked Acorn Squash

Serves 3–4

Ingredients

1 acorn squash
Sunflower or sesame oil, or butter (to coat squash)
Seeds from 1 acorn squash, washed and cleaned of pulp
3 tablespoons Bragg's Liquid Aminos
3 tablespoons sunflower or sesame oil

Instructions

Heat oven to 375°. Cover baking tray with parchment paper (optional).

Peel acorn squash and cut into halves. Clean seeds of pulp. Wash seeds and set aside in a small bowl.

Coat halves of acorn squash with sunflower or sesame oil, or butter, both inside and out. Place halves face down on tray.

Bake for about an hour, or until soft. Put timer on 50 minutes. Check to see if ready by piercing squash skin with a fork. The fork should insert easily.

Combine squash seeds with 3 tablespoons Bragg's and 3 tablespoons sunflower or sesame oil. Spread in a single layer onto a cookie sheet, and bake for 10 to 15 minutes at 375°. Set aside to be used as garnish.

Before serving, cut each baked acorn squash half into quarters (making a total of eight pieces) along the ridged indentations of the squash skin. Serve, using toasted acorn squash seeds as garnish.

Navy Beans with **Curried Fennel**

Serves 4

Ingredients

- 1 cup navy beans (presoaked)
- 4 cups water
- 2 bay leaves
- 2 tablespoons ghee
- 1 tablespoon extra-virgin olive oil
- 1 fennel bulb, minced
- 2 tablespoons fresh fennel leaves
- ½ teaspoon sea salt
- 1½ teaspoons curry powder
- ¼ cup water
- Sea salt
- Black pepper
- 2 teaspoons freshly squeezed lemon juice
- 2 tablespoons fresh parsley

Instructions

Drain water from navy beans and place beans in a pressure cooker. Add 4 cups water and 2 bay leaves. Secure lid and turn to high heat. When pressure cooker comes to full steam, lower heat and simmer for 8 minutes (the time required will vary for different pressure cookers).

Turn off heat. Let pressure cooker cool down until it is safe to open.

Place 2 tablespoons ghee and 1 tablespoon extra-virgin olive oil into a skillet, and melt over medium heat. Add minced fennel bulb, ½ teaspoon sea salt, and 1½ teaspoons curry powder, and lightly sauté. Add ¼ cup of water, cover and simmer about 5 minutes, or until soft.

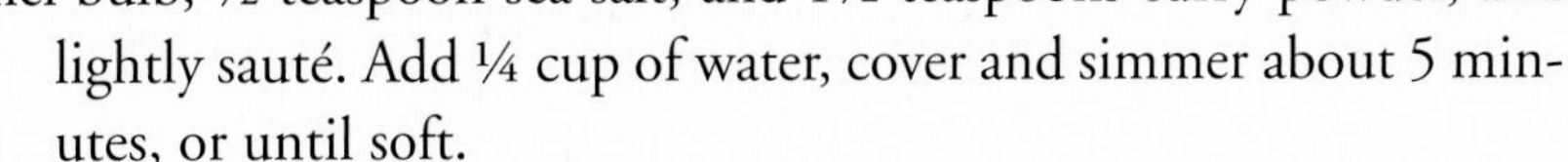

Place cooked navy beans into a large glass bowl. Gently fold in sautéed fennel, and 2 teaspoons fresh lemon juice. Add sea salt and black pepper to taste.

Serve, garnishing with 2 tablespoons fresh fennel leaves and 2 tablespoons fresh parsley.

Tip: The fennel stalks can be saved for making soup stock.

Broccoli with **Ginger Dressing**

Serves 4

Ingredients

- 2 heads of broccoli with stems, rinsed
- ¼ cup ghee, melted
- 2 tablespoons fresh ginger root juice (approx. a 4-inch piece of fresh ginger root)
- 2 teaspoons freshly squeezed lemon juice
- 2 teaspoons Bragg's Liquid Aminos, or tamari

Instructions

Put water in a pot and put on to boil. Peel off thick outer layer of stems from 2 heads broccoli. Cut stems into ¼-inch-thin diagonal slices. Separate the broccoli flowerets into bite sizes.

When water is boiling, place the stem pieces into the steamer basket and steam for a few minutes before adding the flowerets. Steam for 5 to 8 minutes, until bright green and crisp but still tender.

Ginger dressing

Grate the whole, unpeeled ginger root.

Place a small amount of grated ginger into the palm of the hand and squeeze its juice into a bowl. The grated ginger can also be placed on cheesecloth, forming a ball, and the juice squeezed through the cloth into a bowl. Discard the ginger pulp.

Put ¼ cup melted ghee, 2 tablespoons ginger root juice, 2 teaspoons fresh lemon juice, and 2 teaspoons Bragg's (or tamari) into a small glass bowl and whisk briskly with a fork or whisk.

Place steamed broccoli in a bowl and top with ginger dressing.

For Your Health: **Service to others**

Serve others through your cooking. A focus on giving will open your heart and invite the flow of grace. In this way, you and your loved ones will enjoy the food even more.

When I cooked at The Expanding Light Retreat, I noticed that when I focused on cooking with devotion and service to others, people were more likely to approach after the meal to thank me.

Brown Rice with **Oat Groats**

Serves 4–6

Ingredients

- 1 cup short grain brown rice (presoaked)
- ⅓ cup oat groats, or wheat berries (presoaked with rice)
- 2⅓ cups water
- ½ teaspoon Celtic salt

Instructions

Drain soaking water and place 1 cup brown rice and ⅓ cup oat groats into a pressure cooker. Add 2⅓ cups water and ½ teaspoon Celtic salt. Secure lid of pressure cooker and bring to a boil on high heat. Lower heat and simmer for 10 minutes (the time required will vary for different pressure cookers).

Turn heat off. Let pressure cooker cool down until it is safe to open. Fluff rice and groats with a fork and keep covered until serving.

Sautéed Rutabaga, Turnip, and Chard

Serves 4

Ingredients

1 medium-size rutabaga
1 medium-size turnip
3 tablespoons sesame oil
4 stems of chard, minced
4 leaves of chard, cut into thin strips
A few pinches of Celtic salt
Bragg's Liquid Aminos
¼ cup water

Instructions

Peel 1 rutabaga and 1 turnip and slice into ¼-inch rounds.

Heat 3 tablespoons sesame oil in a cast-iron skillet. Add rutabaga, turnip, 4 chopped chard stems, and a few pinches of Celtic salt. Simmer on low heat until softened.

Add 4 slices of chard leaves, a drizzle of Bragg's, and ¼ cup water. Cover and let steam for about 3 minutes. Turn off heat. Keep warm until serving.

Peanut Dressing

Makes ¾ cup

Blend in a blender until smooth:

2 tablespoons sesame oil
2 tablespoons fresh ginger root juice*
¼ teaspoon dried red chili pepper
½ cup (packed) fresh cilantro leaves
4 tablespoons creamy peanut butter
¼ cup water
1 tablespoon Bragg's Liquid Aminos, or tamari
1 teaspoon honey

* See glossary for how to make ginger juice.

Tip: If the peanut butter is too hard, mix it with sesame oil and warm gently, until softened.

Serving Suggestion: A tossed salad with greens, tomatoes, and cucumber is a good accompaniment for this meal.

For Your Health: **Love and respect**

Treat your meal with love and respect. Eat consciously, not absentmindedly. Chewing the food well will help you assimilate the nutrients better. The more you enjoy your food with calm appreciation, the more you will absorb its wholesome vibrations.

Let your cooking be an art form

Try to view cooking as an art form, instead of as a chore. With this attitude, you can enjoy the process *and* the result.

The Buddhist monks, after creating beautiful sand mandalas, erase them. Non-attachment is a good quality to develop. Next time you cook, try to see yourself creating a beautiful piece of art, enjoying the process and the result, and then letting it go without attachment.

Thanksgiving Meal
Ananda Nut Loaf
Mashed Potatoes
Coconut Cranberry Sauce
Baked Yams
Cashew Gravy
Green Beans with Vinaigrette
Pumpkin Pie
*Follow the Bonus Video: www.onlinewithananda.org/holidaymeals
Follow the Video

Thanksgiving

Thanksgiving is a special time
to come together and give thanks
to God, and to family and friends.

Cook with gratitude and love for
all living beings, for the earth,
and for life. Before eating the meal,
you might share a prayer of gratitude.
While eating and socializing,
try to radiate gratitude to
your family and friends, and to God
for all the blessings in your life.

Centering before cooking for Thanksgiving

You can start your meal
preparation with a prayer:

"Beloved God, we thank You for
all Your blessings, but most of all,
we thank You for Your love.
Bless us today as we prepare the
Thanksgiving meal. May the food
be infused with Your joy."

You can affirm while cooking:

"I give thanks to the giver behind
each gift, and to the one Giver
behind all that I receive."*

* From *Affirmations for Self-Healing* by Swami Kriyananda.

Ananda Nut Loaf*

Serves 6–8

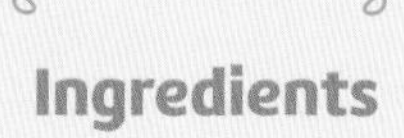

Ingredients

- 3 cups (packed) fresh, whole wheat bread crumbs
- 1 cup (packed) ground walnuts
- 1 cup finely chopped walnuts
- ½ cup nutritional yeast
- 2 tablespoons tamari
- ½ cup tomato juice
- 2 tablespoons sunflower oil
- 2½ large onions, finely chopped
- 3 or 4 large cloves garlic, minced
- 2 eggs
- 1½ cups (packed) grated cheddar cheese
- ¼ to ½ teaspoon sea salt
- ½ teaspoon black pepper
- 2 tablespoons dried parsley or ¾ cup minced fresh parsley

Instructions

Preheat oven to 350°. Combine in a large bowl 3 cups bread crumbs, 1 cup ground walnuts, 1 cup finely chopped walnuts, ½ cup nutritional yeast, 2 tablespoons tamari, and ½ cup tomato juice. Set aside.

Place 2 tablespoons sunflower oil in a large skillet over medium heat. Sauté until translucent 2½ large onions, finely chopped, and 3 or 4 large garlic cloves, minced.

Combine all of the above with 2 well-beaten eggs, 1 cup grated cheddar cheese, ¼ to ½ teaspoon sea salt, ½ teaspoon black pepper, and 2 tablespoons dried parsley (or ¾ cup minced fresh parsley).

Press into well-oiled pan and bake uncovered at 350° for approximately 1 hour. Remove from oven. Sprinkle over top of loaf ½ cup grated cheddar cheese. Bake an additional 10 minutes or until cheese is bubbly. Serve with cashew gravy.

Mashed Potatoes

Serves 6–8

Ingredients

- 4 large russet potatoes
- ¼ cup butter
- ½ to 1 cup milk
- Salt and pepper to taste
- 2 tablespoons minced fresh parsley

Instructions

Peel and cut into cubes 4 large russet potatoes. Place in a pressure cooker with enough water to cover potatoes. Secure lid of pressure cooker and bring to a boil on high heat. Lower heat and simmer for 6 minutes (or as needed, according to pressure cooker used). Turn heat off. Let pressure cooker cool down until it is safe to open.

Drain water and place potatoes in a bowl. Mash potatoes with a potato masher. Add ¼ cup butter. Add ½ to 1 cup of milk, depending upon consistency of potatoes. Add salt and pepper to taste. Garnish with fresh minced parsley.

* Inspired by the *Simply Vegetarian* cookbook by Nancy Mair, Crystal Clarity Publishers.

Coconut Cranberry Sauce*

Serves 6–8

Ingredients

1 cup water
12 ounces fresh cranberries
½ to ¾ cup honey
1 cup grated coconut
4 oranges, peeled, seeded, sectioned, and diced
½ cup chopped walnuts

Instructions

Bring 1 cup water to a boil in a saucepan. Add 12 ounces fresh cranberries and boil until skins "pop" (about 10 minutes). Allow to cool a bit and add ½ to ¾ cup honey.

Pour cranberry mixture into large bowl. Add to bowl and mix well 1 cup grated coconut, 4 diced oranges, and ½ cup chopped walnuts. Serve cold.

Cashew Gravy

Makes 4 cups

Ingredients

⅓ cup butter
1 medium onion, chopped
⅓ cup whole wheat pastry flour
1¼ cups finely ground raw cashews
1 tablespoon plus 1 teaspoon vegetable broth powder
4 cups water
5 tablespoons Bragg's Liquid Aminos, or tamari
¼ cup minced parsley
Black pepper, to taste
¼ teaspoon garlic powder, or to taste

Instructions

Warm a large skillet over medium heat. Add ⅓ cup butter and 1 chopped onion. Sauté a few minutes until onion is translucent.

Stir in ⅓ cup whole wheat pastry flour and 1¼ cups finely ground raw cashews. Stir constantly for 3 minutes.

In a separate saucepan, bring to boil 4 cups of water. Dissolve in 1 tablespoon plus 1 teaspoon vegetable broth powder. Slowly add hot vegetable broth to onion mixture, whisking constantly, until mixture is smooth.

Add 5 tablespoons Bragg's (or tamari), and ¼ teaspoon garlic powder (or more, to taste). Add black pepper, to taste. Bring gravy to a boil, then turn down heat and simmer until thick. Puree in blender in batches to ensure smoothness, or use a hand blender. Before serving, mix in ¼ cup chopped parsley.

* Inspired by the *Simply Vegetarian* cookbook by Nancy Mair, Crystal Clarity Publishers.

Baked Yams*

Serves 6–8

Ingredients

4 medium yams
4 tablespoons coconut oil
2 tablespoons fresh ginger juice
1 teaspoon powdered sugar
2 tablespoons maple syrup

Instructions

Preheat oven to 375°. Peel and cut 4 medium-size yams into 1-inch rounds. Set aside.

Mix in a bowl 4 tablespoons coconut oil, 2 tablespoons fresh ginger juice, 1 teaspoon powdered ginger, and 2 tablespoons maple syrup. Coat the yams with ginger mixture. Place on a baking tray and bake for 30 minutes at 375°, or until the yams are soft and caramelized.

Green Beans with Vinaigrette*

Serves 6–8

Ingredients

4 cups fresh green beans, cut in halves (or 2 pounds frozen green beans)
¼ cup extra-virgin olive oil
1 medium onion, chopped
3 tablespoons fresh lemon juice
1½ teaspoons dried marjoram
½ cup minced fresh parsley
Sea salt, to taste
Black pepper, to taste
½ cup slivered almonds

Instructions

Steam 4 cups fresh green beans (or 2 pounds frozen green beans) until crisp but still tender, about 5 to 10 minutes.

Warm a skillet over medium heat. Add ¼ cup extra-virgin olive oil. When oil is heated add 1 medium onion, chopped. Sauté until golden.

Drain beans and add to onions along with 3 tablespoons fresh lemon juice, 1½ teaspoons dried marjoram, ½ cup fresh minced parsley, and sea salt and black pepper to taste. When serving, garnish with slivered almonds.

* Inspired by the *Simply Vegetarian* cookbook by Nancy Mair, Crystal Clarity Publishers.

Pumpkin Pie

(Gluten-, Sugar-, and Dairy-Free)

Serves 6–8

Ingredients

3 tablespoons sunflower oil
½ cup (for filling) and 3 tablespoons (for crust) maple syrup
⅓ cup arrowroot
⅓ cup quinoa flour
⅔ teaspoon cinnamon (optional)
1 cup ground walnuts
2 eggs
½ cup unsweetened soy milk, or water
¼ teaspoon sea salt
¼ teaspoon ginger powder
¼ teaspoon ground cloves
¾ teaspoon cinnamon
1½ cups of pureed pumpkin, yam, or butternut squash (or one 15-ounce can of Libby's 100% Pure Pumpkin)
Whipped cream or coconut whipped cream (optional). (See page 222.)

Instructions

Preheat oven to 350°.

To make walnut crust, in a large bowl mix 3 tablespoons sunflower oil and 3 tablespoons maple syrup until well blended. Add in ⅓ cup arrowroot, ⅓ cup flour, and ⅔ teaspoon cinnamon. Mix in 1 cup ground walnuts.

Gather dough with hands and press into bottom and sides of lightly oiled 9" glass pie pan. (Avoid bringing crust all the way up to the rim, to prevent burning while baking.)

Bake crust at 350°, for 5 minutes. Remove from oven and let cool for 5 minutes. Now heat oven to 425°.

To make filling, lightly beat 2 eggs in large bowl. Add ½ cup maple syrup and ½ cup unsweetened soymilk, or water.

In a small bowl mix together ¼ teaspoon sea salt, ¼ teaspoon ginger, ¼ teaspoon cloves, and ¾ teaspoon cinnamon. Add spice mixture to egg mixture. Mix well.

To egg and spice mixture add 1½ cups of pureed pumpkin, yam, or butternut squash. Mix well. Pour filling into prebaked walnut crust. Bake at 425° for 15 minutes. Reduce temperature to 350° and bake for an additional 50 to 60 minutes. If the top edges of the pie brown too fast while baking, cover the edges with aluminum foil, and remove the foil after baking.

Allow the pie to cool thoroughly before cutting.

Pie may be served with whipped cream or coconut whipped cream.

Christmas Meal
Baked Acorn Squash with Wild Rice Mix Stuffing
Braised Broccoli with Orange Dressing
Tofu Spinach Pasties
Mushroom Gravy
Maple Walnut Pie
*Follow the Bonus Video: www.onlinewithananda.org/holidaymeals
Follow the Video

Christmas

At our Ananda communities we have both a spiritual and a social Christmas. Our spiritual Christmas is an eight-hour meditation on December 23, during which we try to give birth in our hearts and minds to new consciousness, so that we can offer to others the highest within us. December 25 is our social Christmas, highlighted by a festive community banquet and divine fellowship. Christmas is a very special time for celebrating divine peace and love. As you enjoy this holiday and eat your Christmas meal, try to radiate that peace and love to all.

Centering before cooking for Christmas

Take a few moments to open your heart to the divine consciousness of Christ, and fill your heart with the love of Christ. Cook this meal with the spirit of Christ. You can affirm while cooking:

"I will live in the remembrance of what I am in truth:
bliss infinite! eternal love!"*

* From *Affirmations for Self-Healing* by Swami Kriyananda.

Baked Acorn Squash
with Wild Rice Stuffing

Serves 4–6

Ingredients

2 acorn squash
Sunflower oil—for coating squash and baking seeds
Bragg's Liquid Aminos, or tamari, for baking seeds (optional)
1 cup wild rice mix (presoaked)
½ cup butter (¼ for sautéing shallots, and ¼ for sautéing celery)
1 cup shallots, coarsely chopped
A pinch of Celtic salt
2⅓ cups water
2 tablespoons vegetable broth powder
2 teaspoons dried basil
1 teaspoon dried sage
¾ teaspoon dried thyme
1 cup minced celery
¾ cup minced fresh parsley
⅓ cup toasted sunflower seeds
Salt and pepper to taste

Instructions

Preheat oven to 375°. Wash and dry 2 acorn squash. Cut each in half lengthwise. Scrape out pulp and seeds. Separate pulp from seeds. Wash seeds and set aside.

Cover a baking tray with parchment paper. Coat squash halves inside and out with sunflower oil, and place face down on tray. Bake at 375° for 50 minutes, or until soft when knife is inserted.

Cover another baking tray with parchment paper. Spread squash seeds on tray and drizzle over them sunflower oil and Bragg's (or tamari). Bake at 375° for 10 to 15 minutes, or until lightly toasted. Toasted seeds may be used as garnish for baked squash or other dishes, or as a snack.

In a pressure cooker, melt ¼ cup butter over medium heat. Add 1 cup chopped shallots and a pinch of Celtic salt. Sauté about 5 minutes, until shallots become translucent. Add soaked and drained wild rice mixture, 2⅓ cups water, 2 tablespoons vegetable broth powder, 2 teaspoons dried basil, 1 teaspoon dried sage, and ¾ teaspoon dried thyme.

Secure lid of pressure cooker and bring to a boil on high heat. Lower heat and simmer for 12 minutes (the time required will vary for different pressure cookers). Turn off heat. Let pressure cooker cool until it is safe to open.

While rice is cooking, sauté in a skillet, until soft, 1 cup minced celery in ¼ cup butter. When rice is done, mix together cooked wild rice mixture, sautéed celery, ¾ cup fresh minced parsley, ⅓ cup toasted sunflower seeds, and salt and pepper to taste.

When acorn squash halves are done, fill with wild rice stuffing. Garnish with fresh minced parsley.

Braised Broccoli
with Orange Dressing
Serves 4–6

Ingredients

2 bunches broccoli (about 4 stems)
2 tablespoons extra-virgin olive oil
1½ teaspoons Bragg's Liquid Aminos
1 tablespoon ginger juice*
1 tablespoon honey
3 tablespoons fresh-squeezed orange juice
¼ cup toasted slivered almonds

*See glossary on how to make ginger juice.

Instructions

Wash broccoli and cut into bite-sized flowerets. Peel stems and slice diagonally. Steam flowerets and stems until crisp but still tender.

In a blender, blend together 2 tablespoons extra-virgin olive oil, 1½ teaspoons Bragg's, 1 tablespoon ginger juice, 1 tablespoon honey, and 3 tablespoons orange juice.

Lightly mix dressing into cooked broccoli and sprinkle ¼ cup toasted slivered almonds on top.

Tofu Spinach Pasties
Serves 6–8 (16 small pasties)

Ingredients

Sunflower oil or butter
¼ cup extra-virgin olive oil
1 cup minced onion
4 green onions, minced
10 ounces fresh baby spinach, rinsed, dried, and chopped
1 teaspoon garlic powder
½ cup chopped fresh parsley
7 ounces firm tofu (half a package), crumbled by hand and mashed with fork
2 tablespoons lemon juice
2 teaspoons sea salt
½ teaspoon black pepper
2 sheets puff pastry, thawed (ready-to-bake sheets, 17.3 oz. package)
¾ cup white flour
1 egg

Instructions

Preheat oven to 400°.

Place parchment paper on a baking tray and brush with sunflower oil or butter.

To begin the stuffing, sauté in a large skillet, in ¼ cup extra-virgin olive oil, 1 cup minced onion and 4 minced green onions until soft and lightly browned.

Add baby spinach and sauté until limp (about 2 minutes). Add 1 teaspoon garlic powder and ½ cup fresh chopped parsley. Remove from heat and set aside to cool.

In a large bowl mix half a package (7 ounces) firm tofu—crumbled by hand and mashed with a fork—with 2 tablespoons lemon juice, 2 teaspoons sea salt, and ½ teaspoon black pepper.

Strain spinach mixture in colander to remove excess liquid. (Too much liquid makes the filling too moist for you to seal the pasties easily.) Mix spinach mixture with tofu and set aside.

Unroll 2 sheets puff pastry. Use white flour on countertop to prevent dough from sticking while rolling out, about ¾ cup for 2 sheets puff pastry.

Roll out each puff pastry sheet thin enough to make 6 rounds about 4½ inches in diameter. To cut rounds, use a container with this diameter. (A 32-ounce yogurt container works well.)

After cutting 6 rounds, roll out leftover dough, and cut another two rounds. Each sheet should allow 8 rounds with a little left over for decoration. (See "tip" below.)

Divide the spinach tofu stuffing mixture into 16 portions (about 1½ to 2 tablespoons of stuffing for each pasty). Place the filling on one half of each dough round, leaving a ¼-inch space around the edge. Brush a small amount of water on the edge (just enough to make it sticky; too much makes it slippery), and close the pasty, pressing it together with a fork to seal.

Pierce the top of each pasty with a sharp knife or fork for release of steam while baking. Brush with egg wash (one beaten egg with 1 tablespoon water) or milk. Place in a baking tray on oiled parchment paper and bake at 400° for 15 to 20 minutes or until golden brown. Serve with Mushroom Gravy.

Tip: For decoration, use a star-shaped cookie cutter to cut pieces of any leftover dough. Brush the back of each star with water, and place a star on the top of each pasty before baking.

Mushroom Gravy

Makes 2 ½ cups

Ingredients

4 tablespoons extra-virgin olive oil
3 cups white button mushrooms, thinly sliced
1 tablespoon vegetable broth powder
2 cups water
¼ cup Bragg's Liquid Aminos
2 tablespoons fresh ginger juice* (about a 4-inch piece)
¼ cup cold water
2 tablespoons arrowroot

* See glossary for how to make ginger juice.

Instructions

Sauté in a large skillet, in 4 tablespoons extra-virgin olive oil, 3 cups sliced mushrooms, until golden (about 5 minutes).

In a small pot boil 2 cups water and add 1 tablespoon vegetable broth powder. Add ¼ cup Bragg's Liquid Aminos and 2 tablespoons fresh ginger juice.

Add the sautéed mushrooms to the simmering mixture. Set aside.

Mix in a bowl ¼ cup cold water and 2 tablespoons arrowroot. (One tablespoon of arrowroot will thicken one cup of liquid.) Add to the mushroom mixture and stir frequently until liquid thickens.

Maple Walnut Pie

Serves 8

Ingredients

- 1½ cups whole wheat pastry flour
- ½ teaspoon sea salt
- ⅓ cup sunflower oil
- ¼ cup cold water
- ½ cup butter
- ½ cup agave
- ¼ cup maple syrup
- ¼ teaspoon stevia powder (sweetening equivalent of ¾ cup brown sugar)
- 3 eggs
- 1 teaspoon vanilla
- ½ teaspoon sea salt
- 2 cups chopped walnuts
- Whipped cream, or coconut whipped cream (optional). (See page 222.)

Instructions

Preheat oven to 375°.

To make whole wheat crust:

Mix in a bowl 1½ cups whole wheat pastry flour and ½ teaspoon sea salt. Add ⅓ cup sunflower oil and ¼ cup cold water. Combine, forming into a loose ball of dough.

Place dough in an oiled 9–inch glass pie dish. Press out evenly with fingers, starting from the center, until it fully covers the bottom and sides of the dish. Prick dough on bottom of dish with fork to prevent bubbling.

Bake for 15 minutes at 375°. Remove from oven and set aside.

To make walnut filling:

In a 2-quart saucepan melt ½ cup butter, ½ cup agave, ¼ cup maple syrup, and ¼ teaspoon stevia powder. Turn heat off.

Beat 3 eggs and add slowly to mixture, whisking all the while. While whisking add 1 teaspoon vanilla, ½ teaspoon sea salt, and 2 cups chopped walnuts.

Pour into partially baked pie shell and bake at 375° for 30 minutes or until filling is set.

Allow to cool before cutting. Serve with sweetened whipped cream or coconut whipped cream.

Wheat-Free Nut Crust

Ingredients

3 tablespoons sunflower or other vegetable oil
3 tablespoons maple syrup
⅓ cup arrowroot
⅓ cup quinoa flour
⅔ teaspoon cinnamon (optional)
1 cup ground walnuts

Instructions

Preheat oven to 350°.

Mix 3 tablespoons sunflower oil and 3 tablespoons maple syrup. Add ⅓ cup arrowroot, ⅓ cup quinoa flour, and ⅔ teaspoon cinnamon. Mix in 1 cup ground walnuts.

Press crust into bottom and sides of lightly oiled 9-inch glass pie pan. (Avoid bringing crust all the way up to the rim, to prevent burning while baking.)

Bake crust at 350° for 5 minutes. Let cool for 5 minutes before adding filling.

An alternative crust that uses wheat:

Tender Whole Wheat Pie Crust

Ingredients

¾ cup unbleached white flour
¾ cup whole wheat flour
1 stick (½ cup) cold butter, cut into large pieces
3 tablespoons cold water

Instructions

Preheat oven to 400°. Place in bowl of food processor ¾ cup unbleached white flour, ¾ cup whole wheat flour, and 1 stick cold butter, cut into large pieces.

Turn on food processor. Add, 1 tablespoon at a time, approximately 3 tablespoons of cold water, until a ball of dough forms.

Roll out dough on a lightly floured board. Place in a 9-inch pie plate. Flute the edges and prick bottom and sides with fork. Bake at 400° for 8 to 10 minutes. Allow to cool for 5 minutes before adding filling.

A festive atmosphere can enhance the taste of the food and uplift the spirit

Winter

MENUS

1

Coconut Rice with Sesame Seeds

Tofu Squares with Leeks

Golden Tomato Sauce

2

Winter Vegetable Bean Stew

Barley Bread

3

Split Mung Soup with Herbs

Brown Rice with Wheat Berries

Carrot, Burdock, and Sesame Seeds

4

Valentine's Day

Coconut Squash Soup with Cashews

Tempeh with Broccoli

Apple Pie

5

Seitan with Tahini Dressing

Brown Rice with Gomashio (Sesame-Salt Condiment)

Sautéed Vegetables with Miso-Arrowroot Dressing

6

Wehani Rice

Maple-Sesame Tofu

Sautéed Root Vegetables

7

Vegetable Soup with Tofu

Tricolor Quinoa

Parsley Dressing

Indian Meal

Saffron Rice with Ghee

Saag Paneer

Vegetable Curry

Mango Papaya Chutney

Raita • Lassi • Chai

Variation:

Potato Pea Samosas with Tamarind Raisin Chutney

Dessert: Carrot Halva

8

French Lentil Soup

Sweet Corn Muffins

Winter Meals

The Secret of Radiant Health and Well-Being Is . . .

Happiness within, radiated outward in a sense of well-being to others.
Happiness is the fruit of faith in life, in God, in one's own high potential.

From *Secrets of Radiant Health and Well-Being,* by J. Donald Walters (Swami Kriyananda)

Centering Before Cooking

- In early winter—when the weather is cold, wet, and windy—eat foods that are warming and grounding, like soups, stews, baked root vegetables, and hearty meals. Emphasize warm, moist, heavy foods. Avoid cold foods and drinks, and keep raw foods to a minimum.
- Late in winter, when the weather starts to warm up, you can gradually introduce lighter foods and cooking methods.
- Before cooking, take a few moments to center yourself.
- Take a few deep warm breaths. Feel grounded and centered within yourself. As you cook, focus on infusing the food with loving-kindness and nurturing energy.

Suggested affirmations to use while cooking:

- Centered in myself, I share my love with all.
- I radiate kindness and harmony.
- I am light, ever calm, ever perfect.
- I open to the flow of God's love within me.
- Let my energy be a channel of Thy love and joy.
- I hold in my heart God's peace and joy.
- I am a wave of peace on the ocean of peace.

1 Coconut Rice with Sesame Seeds

Tofu Squares with Leeks
Golden Tomato Sauce

Coconut Rice with Sesame Seeds

Serves 4

Ingredients

1 cup white basmati rice, rinsed
4 tablespoons ghee
2 cups water
1 teaspoon Celtic salt
¼ cup sesame seeds
¼ cup unsweetened shredded coconut

Instructions

Place in a rice cooker 1 cup rinsed white basmati rice and 2 tablespoons melted ghee. Mix well. Add 2 cups water and 1 teaspoon Celtic salt. Cook until done, then remove cover and fluff. Cover until serving.

Place 2 tablespoons ghee in a skillet over low heat. Add ¼ cup sesame seeds and ¼ cup unsweetened shredded coconut. Sauté, stirring continuously, until darkened and fragrant. Pour over the cooked rice and toss to mix.

Tofu Squares with Leeks

Serves 4

Ingredients

- 1 pound firm tofu (one 14–16 oz. package)
- 6 tablespoons arrowroot* (or cornstarch)
- 6 tablespoons sesame oil
- 1 leek, minced (white and pale green parts), about 3 cups
- 1 tablespoon fresh ginger root, peeled and grated
- 3 tablespoons Bragg's Liquid Aminos, or tamari
- 1½ teaspoons maple syrup
- ½ cup water

* See glossary.

Instructions

Using paper towels, pat 1 pound tofu cube to remove excess water. Cut cube in half. Cut each half into 8 squares, 2 x 2 x ½-inch (16 squares).

Spoon 3 tablespoons of arrowroot (or cornstarch) onto a plate. Coat half of the tofu (8 pieces) on all sides. Place coated tofu on a plate.

Using 3 more tablespoons of arrowroot (or cornstarch), repeat for second batch of tofu (remaining 8 pieces).

Add 2 tablespoons sesame oil to a large skillet over medium heat. Sauté half of tofu pieces until crisp and golden on the outside. Remove to plate.

Using 2 more tablespoons sesame oil, repeat for second batch of tofu.

Place all pieces of tofu in the skillet, cover and set aside.

In a small saucepan heat 2 tablespoons sesame oil. Add 1 minced leek and 1 tablespoon grated ginger. Sauté for 5 minutes.

Add 3 tablespoons Bragg's (or tamari), 1½ teaspoons maple syrup, and ½ cup water. Bring to a boil and simmer for 3 minutes.

Fold leek mixture into sautéed tofu in a skillet, cover and simmer for 5 minutes.

Turn heat off and let sit another 5 minutes to absorb flavors. Serve warm.

Golden Tomato Sauce

Makes 1¼ cups. Serves 3–4.

Ingredients

2 tablespoons sunflower oil
½ medium-size red onion, minced (about ½ cup)
1 large clove garlic, peeled and minced
2 medium-size ripe tomatoes, peeled and cut into small cubes
¼ cup water
⅓ cup raw butternut squash, peeled and grated
2 tablespoons extra-virgin olive oil
½ teaspoon dried basil
1 teaspoon nutritional yeast
¼ teaspoon salt
A few fresh basil leaves

Instructions

Place 2 tablespoons sunflower oil in a small saucepan over medium heat. Add ½ cup minced red onion and 1 clove minced garlic. Sauté for about 5 minutes.

Mix in 2 medium-size tomatoes (peeled and cubed). Simmer for 8 minutes. Remove from heat.

Blend tomato mixture in a blender until smooth.

Return to saucepan and add ¼ cup water, ⅓ cup grated butternut squash, 2 tablespoons extra-virgin olive oil, ½ teaspoon dried basil, 1 teaspoon nutritional yeast, and ¼ teaspoon salt.

Cover and simmer for 5 minutes. Turn off heat and let sit for 5 minutes to absorb flavors.

Serve warm. Garnish with fresh basil.

Tip: How to peel the skin of a tomato: Tomatoes have very tight skins. The only way to peel off the skin without losing too much of the flesh is to quick boil them.

Bring a pot of water to a boil. At the base of the tomato, cut an "X" with a sharp paring knife. Put tomato into boiling water and simmer for a few minutes. Take tomato out with tongs and place in a bowl of iced water to cool off. Place tomato on a towel, dry the surface of the tomato and peel off the skin, starting at cuts at base.

For Your Health: Gratitude

The Bhagavad Gita (the Hindu Bible) says that when we offer even a leaf with love, God is pleased. The most important ingredient in any recipe is our consciousness, the attitude we put into our cooking. The more we cook with love and gratitude, the more we will be able to infuse the food with uplifting energy and vitality.

Winter Vegetable Bean Stew

Serves 4–5

Instructions

Place rinsed, presoaked navy beans in a pressure cooker with 4 cups water and 2 bay leaves. Secure lid of pressure cooker and bring to a boil on high heat. Lower heat and simmer for 3 minutes (the time required will vary for different pressure cookers).

Turn heat off. Let pressure cooker cool down until it is safe to open. Set aside.

While the beans are cooking in the pressure cooker, heat 3 tablespoons extra-virgin olive oil in a skillet over medium heat. Add 1 minced leek, 1 cup minced onion, and 1½ teaspoons garlic powder. Sauté for 5 minutes.

Ingredients

1 cup navy beans (presoaked)
4 cups water
2 bay leaves
3 tablespoons extra-virgin olive oil
1 leek, minced (white and pale-green parts), about 2½ cups
1 cup minced onion
1½ teaspoons garlic powder
2 tablespoons vegetable broth powder
2½ cups butternut squash, peeled, seeded, and cut into 1-inch cubes
1 red bell pepper, seeded and cut into ½-inch cubes
1½ teaspoons dried sage powder
1 cup water
4 kale leaves, chopped into bite-sized pieces
Kale stems, cut into thin slices
1½ teaspoons sea salt, or to taste
Black pepper to taste (use freshly ground)

When beans are done, remove the bay leaves and add to pressure cooker 2 tablespoons vegetable broth powder, the sautéed leek mixture, 2½ cups butternut squash cubes, 1 red bell pepper cubed, 1½ teaspoons dried sage powder, 1 cup water, 4 chopped kale leaves, and sliced kale stems.

Secure lid of pressure cooker and bring to a boil on high heat. Lower heat and simmer for 2 minutes (the time required will vary for different pressure cookers).

Turn heat off. Let pressure cooker cool down until it is safe to open.

After soup is done, add 1½ teaspoons sea salt, or to taste, and freshly ground black pepper, to taste.

Barley Bread

A quick, nonfat, crusty country bread

Makes 4 small loaves. Serves 8–10.

Ingredients

1½ cups whole wheat flour
1 cup unbleached white flour
1 cup barley flour
1 teaspoon sea salt
1 teaspoon baking soda
1 teaspoon baking powder
2 tablespoons sesame seeds (optional: different nuts, seeds, or raisins may be added to give different flavors)
2 cups buttermilk, or 2½ cups plain yogurt

Instructions

Preheat oven to 375°.

Mix in a large bowl 1½ cups whole wheat flour, 1 cup unbleached white flour, 1 cup barley flour, 1 teaspoon sea salt, 1 teaspoon baking soda, 1 teaspoon baking powder, and 2 tablespoons sesame seeds.

Make an indentation in the middle of the bowl and pour in 2 cups buttermilk (or 2½ cups plain yogurt). With a spatula fold the flour into the buttermilk. The dough should be soft.

To shape the loaves:

Version 1:

For a crusty, country surface (makes a "dry" loaf)

Place the dough on a countertop. Put white flour on your hands and on the countertop to prevent sticking. Cut dough into four sections. Pat each section with white flour. Form a baguette-shaped loaf and place on a baking tray that is covered with parchment paper. (The bread tends to flatten as it cooks.) Using a sharp knife, lightly make diagonal slits on surface of each loaf.

Version 2:

Makes a "moist" loaf

With wet hands, place dough on oiled baking tray. Form into 4 baguette-shaped loaves. Using sharp knife, lightly make diagonal slits on the surface of each loaf.

Bake at 375° for 30–40 minutes, until golden-brown. Cool completely, then slice thin.

Tip: This bread freezes well. Slice, and place slices in a ziplock bag in the freezer. Slices can be removed individually, to be thawed or toasted.

For Your Health: **Positive energy**

While preparing food, try to keep your energy positive and uplifted. The quality of the energy you put into your cooking will be reflected in the food itself and in how you and others feel after eating it.

While cooking, to uplift your energy, you can mentally repeat a positive affirmation. A simple affirmation such as "I am positive, energetic, enthusiastic," or "I am calm and joyful" might help you. Repeat it with energy and sincerity, and try to feel the positive vibrations flowing through you into the food.

3 Split Mung Soup with Herbs

Brown Rice with Wheat Berries
Carrot, Burdock, and Sesame Seeds

Split Mung Soup with **Herbs**

Serves 5–6

Ingredients

3 tablespoons ghee
1 teaspoon mustard seeds
1 cup minced onion
2 tablespoons peeled and grated ginger
½ teaspoon turmeric powder
1 teaspoon fennel powder
1 teaspoon coriander powder
½ teaspoon cumin powder
1 teaspoon dried basil
¼ teaspoon garam masala*
1 cup rinsed split mung beans
5 cups water
1 tablespoon vegetable broth powder
2 stalks celery, chopped
1½ cups carrot, peeled and minced (about 2 carrots)
1 cup chopped green cabbage
4 collard-green leaves, without stems, chopped
1½ teaspoons sea salt
1½ teaspoons fresh lemon juice

* See glossary.

Instructions

Place 3 tablespoons ghee into a pressure cooker. Heat ghee over medium heat, adding 1 teaspoon mustard seeds. Wait for mustard seeds to "pop."

Mix in 1 cup minced onion, 2 tablespoons peeled and grated ginger, ½ teaspoon turmeric powder, 1 teaspoon fennel powder, 1 teaspoon coriander powder, ½ teaspoon cumin powder, 1 teaspoon dried basil, and ¼ teaspoon garam masala. Sauté this mix for a few minutes.

Add 5 cups water, 1 cup rinsed split mung beans, 1 tablespoon vegetable broth powder, 2 stalks chopped celery, 1½ cups peeled and minced carrots, 1 cup chopped green cabbage, and 4 chopped collard-green leaves. Secure lid of pressure cooker and bring to a boil. When pressure cooker reaches full steam, lower heat and simmer for 5 minutes (the time required will vary for different pressure cookers). Turn off heat. Let pressure cooker cool until it is safe to open.

Add 1½ teaspoons sea salt and 1½ teaspoons fresh lemon juice.

Blend soup in a blender, or with hand blender, until smooth.

Brown Rice with Wheat Berries

Serves 4–6

Ingredients

1 cup short grain brown rice (presoaked)
⅓ cup wheat berries* (presoaked with brown rice)
2⅓ cups water
½ teaspoon Celtic salt

* See glossary.

Instructions

Drain soaking water from rice and wheat berries, rinse, and place in pressure cooker with 2⅓ cups water and ½ teaspoon Celtic salt.

Secure lid of pressure cooker and bring to a boil on high heat. Lower heat and simmer for 10 minutes (the time required will vary for different pressure cookers).Turn off heat. Let pressure cooker cool down until it is safe to open.

Fluff rice and wheat berries with a fork and keep covered until serving.

Carrot, Burdock, and Sesame Seeds

Serves 3–4

Ingredients

2 burdock roots, about 12–18 inches each
2 medium-size carrots
2 tablespoons sesame oil
⅓ cup water
Bragg's Liquid Aminos, or tamari
2 tablespoons sesame seeds, tan or black
2 tablespoons minced parsley

Instructions

Scrub 2 burdock roots with a vegetable brush to remove brown skin, or peel with a vegetable peeler. Scrub or peel 2 carrots.

Cut burdock and carrots in half, lengthwise, then slice each half, diagonally, into matchsticks.

Heat 2 tablespoons sesame oil in a skillet. Add burdock and sauté for 3 minutes. Add carrots and sauté for a further 3 minutes.

Add ⅓ cup water (or more, if needed). Cover and simmer for about 10 minutes, or until water is absorbed. Drizzle Bragg's or tamari over vegetables.

Cover and let sit for 5 to 10 minutes. Add more Bragg's or tamari to taste if needed.

Place a small skillet over medium heat. In dry skillet place 2 tablespoons sesame seeds. Toast, turning often, until lightly browned.

Fold toasted sesame seeds into burdock and carrots.

Serve with a garnish of minced parsley.

Tip: There is no real difference in taste or nutritional value between white and black sesame seeds. If using black sesame seeds, add just before serving, as they tend to darken the color of vegetables

For Your Health: **Eat with the seasons**

During the winter, when it's cold and windy, the body is more vulnerable and needs to be well nourished. It's important to keep the body warm and stable. By eating grounding and warming foods, you can help your body stay healthy and full of vitality.

Happy Valentine's Day!

On Valentine's Day make something special for someone you love: a spouse, a friend, a mother or father, anyone you want to honor and give love to. While you prepare the meal, send rays of love from your heart to this person. Give thanks to God for bringing him or her into your life.

Centering for Valentine's Day

Before you start cooking, center yourself in your heart. Take a few deep, purifying breaths, then visualize rays of divine love flowing outward from your heart and blessing those for whom you are cooking. You can extend love and blessings to all living beings.

Affirm:

"I will love others as extensions of my own Self, and of the love I feel from God."*

As you cook, let love flow through your hands to infuse the food you are preparing, that it nurture and comfort those who eat it.

* From *Affirmations for Self-Healing*, by Swami Kriyananda.

Coconut Squash Soup with Cashews

Serves 5–6

Ingredients

2 tablespoons ghee or coconut oil
1 cup minced onion
1 celery stalk, minced
1 tablespoon fresh ginger, peeled and grated
A pinch of Celtic salt
2 cups carrots, cut into quarter rounds
2 tablespoons vegetable broth powder
5 cups butternut squash, cut into 1-inch cubes (1 small to medium butternut squash)
2½ cups water
1 14-ounce can unsweetened coconut milk
1 cup raw cashews
1 teaspoon sea salt
Sea salt to taste
Toasted cashews for garnish

Instructions

In a pressure cooker, warm 2 tablespoons ghee on medium heat. Add 1 cup minced onion, 1 minced celery stalk, 1 tablespoon fresh grated ginger, and a pinch of Celtic salt. Sauté for a few minutes.

Add 2 cups cut carrots, 5 cups cubed butternut squash, 2 tablespoons vegetable broth powder, and 2½ cups water. Secure lid of pressure cooker and bring to a boil on high heat. Lower heat and simmer for 5 minutes (the time required will vary for different pressure cookers).

Turn off heat. Let pressure cooker cool down until it is safe to open. Then add 1 can unsweetened coconut milk, 1 cup raw cashews, and 1 teaspoon sea salt.

Puree soup in a blender, or with an immersion blender, until smooth. Add salt to taste. Garnish with toasted cashews.

Variation: Instead of toasted cashews, sauté some sliced button mushrooms in ghee until golden, and sprinkle on top of soup before serving.

Tempeh with **Broccoli**

Serves 4

Ingredients

2 8-ounce packages plain tempeh, cut into ½-inch cubes
¼ cup coconut oil
A drizzle of Bragg's Liquid Aminos
A squeeze of lemon juice
1–2 tablespoons fresh ginger juice*
4 heads broccoli, rinsed and cut into bite-sized flowerets
1 cup water
Stems of 4 heads broccoli, peeled and cut into ¼-inch diagonal slices

*See glossary on how to make ginger juice.

Instructions

In a large skillet, heat ¼ cup coconut oil on low heat. Add tempeh cubes, in one layer, and sauté on low heat until brown (about 8–10 minutes). Add a drizzle of Bragg's, a squeeze of lemon juice, and 1–2 tablespoons fresh ginger juice.* Set aside.

In a steamer pot, boil about 1 cup water. First add to steamer basket the sliced broccoli stem pieces. After a few minutes, add broccoli flowerets. Steam for 5 to 8 minutes, until bright green and crisp but still tender.

After the broccoli is ready, place in a serving bowl and sprinkle with extra-virgin olive oil, sea salt, and a squeeze of lemon juice. Either mix with tempeh cubes or serve separately.

Variation: You can use any other green vegetable, such as kale or bok choy.

Ingredients

2¼ cups whole wheat pastry flour
1½ teaspoons sea salt
½ cup plus 1 tablespoon sunflower oil
⅓ cup cold water
3 sweet red apples, cored and cut into ¼-inch slices
1 tart green apple, cored and cut into ¼-inch slices
3 tablespoons sunflower oil
A few pinches of Celtic salt
1 teaspoon cinnamon
1 pinch nutmeg
½ cup maple syrup or agave
¼ cup raisins (optional)
½ cup chopped walnuts
1½ tablespoons fresh lemon juice
2 tablespoons sunflower oil or milk
A sprinkle of cinnamon
Whipped cream, or coconut whipped cream (optional)
(See page 222.)

Apple Pie

Serves 6

Instructions

To form dough, mix in a bowl 2¼ cups whole wheat pastry flour, 1½ teaspoons sea salt, ½ cup plus 1 tablespoon sunflower oil, and ⅓ cup cold water.

Cut dough into two pieces (⅔ and ⅓). Save ⅓ for top crust. Place ⅔ of dough in an oiled 9-inch glass pie dish. Press out evenly with fingers, starting from the center until it fully covers bottom and sides of baking dish. Prick bottom of dough with fork to prevent bubbling.

Bake for 15 minutes at 375°. Remove from oven and set aside. Reduce oven temperature to 350°.

In a pot, warm 3 tablespoons sunflower oil on medium heat. Add sliced apples and a few pinches of Celtic salt, and sauté briefly. Cover pot and simmer on low heat until apple slices are soft (about 10 minutes).

Add to apples: 1 teaspoon cinnamon, a pinch of nutmeg, ½ cup maple syrup, ¼ cup raisins, ½ cup chopped walnuts, and 1½ tablespoons fresh lemon juice.

Place apple mixture on top of pie crust. Take remainder of dough and roll on flat surface. Use heart-shaped cookie cutters to make thin heart-shaped dough pieces. Place on top of apples in desired arrangement. Brush dough with oil or milk and sprinkle with ground cinnamon. Bake at 350° for 30 minutes. Serve with whipped cream or coconut whipped cream.

Tip: For this pie the dough recipe was multiplied by 1½. The original, single-crust recipe calls for 1½ cups whole wheat pastry flower, 1 teaspoon sea salt, ⅓ cup sunflower oil, and ¼ cup cold water.

Variation: *Gluten-Free, Wheat-Free Walnut Crust*

Ingredients

- 3 tablespoons sunflower oil
- 3 tablespoons maple syrup
- ⅓ cup arrowroot
- ⅓ cup quinoa flour
- ½ teaspoon cinnamon (optional)
- 1 cup ground walnuts

Instructions

In a large bowl mix 3 tablespoons sunflower oil and 3 tablespoons maple syrup until well blended. Add in ⅓ cup arrowroot, ⅓ cup quinoa flour, and ½ teaspoon cinnamon. Mix in 1 cup ground walnuts.

Press dough onto bottom and sides of lightly oiled 9-inch glass pie pan. (To prevent burning while baking, avoid bringing crust all the way up to rim.)

Note: This amount will make only the bottom crust. If topping over the apple filling is desired, double recipe and crumble on top of the apples, sprinkle with ground cinnamon, and drizzle melted butter or oil to keep moist.

Bake crust at 350° for 5 minutes. Remove from oven and let cool for 5 minutes.

Happy Valentine's Day!

Seitan with **Tahini Dressing**

Seitan is a wheat gluten, made from whole wheat flour and water. Serves 3–4

Ingredients

- 1 cup wheat gluten flour*
- ½ teaspoon garlic powder, or more, to taste
- ½ teaspoon ginger powder, or more, to taste
- 1½ tablespoons Bragg's Liquid Aminos, or tamari
- 1½ teaspoons sesame oil
- ¾ cup water
- 4 cups water
- ¼ cup Bragg's Liquid Aminos, or tamari
- 4 slices fresh, unpeeled ginger
- 2 tablespoons sesame or sunflower oil

* See "seitan" in glossary.

Instructions

In a small bowl mix 1 cup wheat gluten flour, ½ teaspoon garlic powder, and ½ teaspoon ginger powder. In a separate bowl mix 1½ tablespoons Bragg's (or tamari), 1½ teaspoons sesame oil, and ¾ cup water.

Add gluten mixture to water mixture and stir until flour is well absorbed, and a ball of dough can be formed with the hands. Add to a pot 4 cups water, ¼ cup Bragg's (or tamari), 4 slices ginger, and the ball of gluten dough.

Bring to a boil and simmer for about 15 minutes. With tongs or spatula, turn seitan halfway through. Remove seitan from pot with a strainer or slotted spoon. Cool for a few minutes. (Water may be saved to cook grains or legumes, or as soup stock.)

Slice into thin slices. Heat sesame oil or sunflower oil in a skillet on medium heat. Sauté seitan, drizzling Bragg's on top. Serve with Tahini Dressing.

Tip: If making a large amount of seitan, brush tops of slices with oil, then bake in oven at 350° until outside is crisp.

Tahini Dressing

Makes 1¾ cups

Place into a blender and blend until smooth:

- ¾ cup water
- ¼ cup extra-virgin olive oil
- ½ cup tahini (roasted)
- 1 tablespoon maple syrup, or a pinch of stevia powder
- 2 teaspoons Bragg's Liquid Aminos, or tamari
- ½ teaspoon garlic powder
- ½ teaspoon dried dill or 1½ teaspoons fresh dill (optional)
- ¼ teaspoon sea salt
- 1 pinch black pepper
- ¼ cup (packed) parsley leaves (optional)
- ¼ cup fresh-squeezed lemon juice

Brown Rice

Serves 3–4

Ingredients

- 1 cup long grain brown rice, presoaked
- 2 cups water
- A pinch of Celtic salt

Instructions

Rinse presoaked rice and add to a pressure cooker with 2 cups water, and a pinch of Celtic salt. Secure lid of pressure cooker and bring to a boil on high heat. Lower heat and simmer for 10 minutes (the time required will vary for different pressure cookers). Turn off heat. Let pressure cooker cool down until it is safe to open. Fluff rice with a fork before serving.

Gomashio

A tasty condiment, gomashio is used in Japanese cuisine.

Makes ⅓ cup

Ingredients

- 5 tablespoons sesame seeds
- 1 tablespoon sea salt

Instructions

In a small skillet on medium heat, lightly toast 5 tablespoons sesame seeds. Using a mortar and pestle, place toasted sesame seeds in bowl with 1 tablespoon sea salt, and crush until seeds are ground. A blender may also be used, gently pulsing a few times until sesame seeds are ground. After you grind the mixture, place in a shaker.

Tip: Gomashio is a great substitute for salt. The ratio of sesame seeds to salt varies according to taste and diet, generally ranging between 5:1 (5 parts sesame seeds to 1 part salt) and 15:1.

Ingredients

3 tablespoons sesame oil
1 burdock, cut into matchsticks (about ½ cup)
1 medium-size yellow beet, cut into quarter rounds, about ¼-inch thick
A few pinches of Celtic salt
3 cups chopped green cabbage
¾ cup sliced shiitake mushroom (if dried, soak for 2 hours beforehand, or overnight)
1 cup carrot, cut into half rounds, about ¼-inch thick
2 broccoli, with stems
⅓ cup of water
1 tablespoon Bragg's Liquid Aminos
1 tablespoon miso* paste (mellow white)
¼ cup water
1 tablespoon arrowroot

* See glossary.

Sautéed Vegetables with Miso-Arrowroot Dressing

Serves 4–5

Instructions

Heat 3 tablespoons sesame oil in a cast-iron skillet on medium heat. Sauté 1 sliced burdock and 1 sliced yellow beet, with a pinch of Celtic salt.

Add 3 cups chopped green cabbage and another pinch of Celtic salt. Cover and let soften.

Add shiitake mushroom slices, 1 cup sliced carrot, and the flowerets and stems (peeled and sliced thin diagonally) of 2 broccoli. Add ⅓ cup water and 1 tablespoon Bragg's. Cover and let steam on low heat for about 10 minutes, or until soft enough for your liking.

To make miso-arrowroot sauce, mix in a small bowl 1 tablespoon mellow white miso paste, ¼ cup water, and 1 tablespoon arrowroot. Strain sauce through a strainer for smooth consistency.

When the vegetables are cooked, make an indentation in the center of them, add sauce and let the heat thicken it, then fold the sauce into the vegetables.

For Your Health: How much to eat?

Paramhansa Yogananda, a great yoga master, gave a good tip regarding how much to eat at each meal. He said: "At breakfast eat like a prince; at lunch eat like a king; and at dinner eat like a pauper."

Wehani Rice

Serves 3–4

Ingredients

1 cup Wehani rice, rinsed
3 cups water
2½ cups water
½ teaspoon Celtic salt

Instructions

Soak 1 cup rinsed Wehani rice overnight in 3 cups water.

The next day put 2½ cups water, soaked Wehani rice, and ½ teaspoon Celtic salt in a pressure cooker. Secure lid of pressure cooker and bring to a boil on high heat. Lower heat and simmer for 12 minutes (the time required will vary for different pressure cookers). Turn off heat. Let pressure cooker cool down until it is safe to open. Rice should be soft and tender.

Tip: If you can't find Wehani rice, substitute long grain brown rice.

Maple-Sesame Tofu

Serves 3–4

Ingredients

2 tablespoons maple syrup
3 tablespoons Bragg's Liquid Aminos, or tamari
2 tablespoons sunflower oil
1 tablespoon fresh ginger juice*
1 tablespoon sesame seeds
1 14-ounce package firm tofu, cut in triangles

* See glossary for how to make ginger juice.

Instructions

Preheat oven to 350°. In a bowl mix 2 tablespoons maple syrup, 3 tablespoons Bragg's (or tamari), 2 tablespoons sunflower oil, 1 tablespoon fresh ginger juice,* and 1 tablespoon sesame seeds.

Drain a 14-ounce package of firm tofu. Pat dry. Slice the tofu lengthwise into 4 equal pieces the same size as the original, except ¼ as thick. Slice each piece in half, and each half in half, for a total of 16 squares. Cut each one diagonally, for a total of 32 triangles.

Arrange the tofu triangles on a baking pan about 1 inch apart. Pour the mixture over the tofu and allow to marinate for 60 minutes. Turn the pieces over and bake at 350° for approximately 20 minutes. Serve hot or cold.

Sautéed Root Vegetables

Serves 3–4

Instructions

In a cast-iron skillet, sauté 2 tablespoons sesame oil, 2 tablespoons ghee, 1 cup minced onion, a pinch of Celtic salt, and cut stems of Russian kale (optional).

Ingredients

2 tablespoons sesame oil
2 tablespoons ghee
1 cup minced onion
A pinch of Celtic salt
Stems of Russian kale, cut diagonally into thin strips (optional)
1 cup turnip, cut into ½-inch cubes
1 cup rutabaga, cut into ½-inch cubes
1 cup carrot, cut into quarter rounds, sliced ¼-inch thick
A few pinches of Celtic salt
1 tablespoon Bragg's Liquid Aminos
⅓ cup water
1 teaspoon oregano (optional)
3 cups (packed) Russian kale leaves, cut into thin strips

Add 1 cup cubed turnip, 1 cup cubed rutabaga, 1 cup sliced carrot, and a few pinches of Celtic salt. Sauté on low heat.

Sprinkle on 1 tablespoon Bragg's, ⅓ cup water, and 1 teaspoon oregano (optional). Cover and let simmer until veggies start to soften (about 10 minutes).

Add 3 cups of cut Russian kale. Cover and let simmer until veggies are soft (an additional 5–10 minutes).

For Your Health: Good taste and visual appeal

You can use food as a source of healing, strength, and nourishment—and at the same time be creative with it. When you make food tasty and visually appealing to the senses, you'll enjoy what you eat, and the body will absorb more nutrients from the food.

Vegetable Soup with Tofu

Serves 4

Ingredients

½ ounce of dried shiitake mushroom, sliced and soaked (about ¾ cup)
1 14-ounce package firm tofu, rinsed and cubed
Bragg's Liquid Aminos
3 tablespoons sesame oil
1 cup minced red onion
A pinch of Celtic salt
2 cups chopped green cabbage
1 medium carrot, cut into half rounds, about ¼-inch thick
3 cups butternut squash, cut into 1-inch cubes
4 tablespoons ginger, peeled and grated
¼ cup dulse,* cut into 1-inch pieces
6 cups water
2 tablespoons vegetable broth powder
1 teaspoon dried oregano
¼ teaspoon cayenne (optional)
1 teaspoon Celtic salt, or to taste

* See glossary.

Instructions

Soak for 2 hours in boiling water, or overnight in room temperature water, ½ ounce dried, sliced shiitake mushrooms.

On a cutting board cut 1 package firm, rinsed tofu into ½-inch cubes. Place tofu cubes on a flat plate and drizzle with Bragg's. Let sit for about 10 minutes before adding to soup.

In a pressure cooker, warm 3 tablespoons sesame oil on medium heat. Add 1 cup minced red onion and a pinch of Celtic salt and sauté for a few minutes. Add 2 cups of chopped green cabbage, 1 cut carrot, and soaked shiitake mushrooms, and sauté for another few minutes. Next add 3 cups cubed butternut squash, 4 tablespoons peeled and grated ginger, cubed tofu, ¼ cup cut dulse, 6 cups water, 2 tablespoons vegetable broth powder, and 1 teaspoon dried oregano. Add ¼ teaspoon cayenne if desired.

Secure lid of pressure cooker and bring to a boil on high heat. Lower heat and simmer for 5 minutes (the time required will vary for different pressure cookers). Turn off heat. Let pressure cooker cool down until it is safe to open. After the soup is done, add 1 teaspoon Celtic salt or to taste.

Tricolor Quinoa

Serves 4

Ingredients

1 cup tricolor quinoa, rinsed
2⅓ cups water
½ teaspoon Celtic salt

Instructions

Put 1 cup of tricolor quinoa in a bowl and cover with warm water. Let sit for 5 minutes, then rinse.

Oil the insert bowl of an electric rice cooker. Place rinsed quinoa into the rice cooker bowl with 2⅓ cups water and ½ teaspoon Celtic salt and mix well. Cover with lid, turn rice cooker on, and cook until ready. (Most rice cookers will take about 20 minutes.) When cooked, fluff with a wooden spoon. Let sit for a few minutes, covered, before serving.

Tip: You can substitute regular quinoa for tricolor quinoa. Quinoa kernels have a waxy protective coating, which gives the quinoa a bitter taste. Rinsing the quinoa before cooking will get rid of the bitter coating.

Parsley Dressing

Serves 4

Ingredients

½ cup extra-virgin olive oil
1 cup (packed) fresh parsley leaves
1 teaspoon sea salt

Instructions

In a blender mix ½ cup extra-virgin olive oil, 1 cup fresh parsley leaves, and 1 teaspoon sea salt. Serve with quinoa.

For Your Health: Make healthy choices in what you eat

Paramhansa Yogananda taught that one-third of what we eat keeps us alive, the other two-thirds keeps the doctors alive. He said: "Since you have to eat, why not eat rightly?" Our thoughts, actions, and health are greatly influenced by the foods we eat. The more you make good choices in what you eat, the healthier and happier you will be.

French Lentil Soup

Serves 4–5

Ingredients

1 cup French lentils, sorted and rinsed
4 cups water
2 bay leaves
3 tablespoons sunflower oil
1 cup minced onion
2 celery stalks, cut in thin (¼-inch) diagonals
2 cups (packed) chopped Russian kale leaves (without stems)
Stems of kale, cut into thin diagonal strips (optional)
2 cups chopped Savoy cabbage
A few pinches of Celtic salt
2 tablespoons vegetable broth powder
4 cups water
2 cups yam, cut into ½-inch cubes
2 tablespoons Bragg's Liquid Aminos, or to taste
1 teaspoon curry powder (optional)

Instructions

Place in a pressure cooker 1 cup French lentils, 4 cups water, and 2 bay leaves. Secure lid of pressure cooker and bring to a boil on high heat. Lower heat and simmer for 5 minutes (the time required will vary for different pressure cookers).

Turn off heat. Let pressure cooker cool down until it is safe to open.

Put 3 tablespoons sunflower oil in a skillet on medium heat. Add 1 cup onion, 2 sliced celery stalks, kale stems (save leaves for later in recipe), 2 cups chopped Savoy cabbage, and a few pinches of Celtic salt. Sauté until onions are translucent.

After you open the pressure cooker, add 2 tablespoons vegetable broth powder, the sautéed vegetables, 4 cups water, 2 cups cubed yam, and 2 cups chopped kale leaves.

Secure the lid, then bring pressure cooker to a boil once again. Lower heat and simmer for 3 minutes (the time required will vary for different pressure cookers). Turn off heat. Let pressure cooker cool down until it is safe to open. Add to soup 2 tablespoons Bragg's, or to taste. For spicier flavor, add 1 teaspoon of curry powder.

Tip: Before cooking French lentils, sort them for little stones and other debris and rinse them. You don't need to soak them, especially if you are using a pressure cooker.

Sweet Corn Muffins

These sweet corn muffins are light, and dairy- and sugar-free.

Makes 12 muffins

Ingredients

2 eggs, beaten
⅓ cup sunflower oil, or melted butter
⅓ cup agave, or maple syrup
1 cup yellow cornmeal
1 cup whole wheat pastry flour
2 teaspoons baking powder
⅔ cup rice milk
⅓ cup sunflower oil

Instructions

Preheat oven to 350°. In a large bowl mix 2 beaten eggs, ⅓ cup sunflower oil, and ⅓ cup agave.

In a small bowl sift together 1 cup yellow cornmeal, 1 cup whole wheat pastry flour, and 2 teaspoons baking powder.

Add dry ingredients to wet ingredients. Add ⅔ cup rice milk.

Oil muffin tin lightly with sunflower oil and spoon in batter. Each compartment will be about half full. Bake at 350° for 20 minutes, or until tops are lightly golden and an inserted toothpick comes out clean.

For Your Health: **Healthy comfort food**

What is your comfort food? Make sure that it is good for you. Ask the food: Can you comfort me and nourish me? Can you relax and uplift my spirits? If the answer is yes, your choice will give you true comfort.

Indian Meal

Saffron Rice with Ghee
Saag Paneer • Vegetable Curry
Mango Papaya Chutney
Raita • Lassi • Chai

Variation: Potato Pea Samosas with Tamarind Raisin Chutney *Dessert:* Carrot Halva

Saffron Rice with **Ghee**

Serves 4–5

Ingredients

Basmati rice
2 tablespoons ghee
½ teaspoon saffron threads

Instructions

Boil 6 cups of water. Meanwhile, wash the rice by putting it in a bowl of water and massaging it until, after repeated washings, the water remains clear.

Add the drained rice to the boiling water and keep the heat high so there is a light, rolling boil for about 15 minutes.

Add 2 cups of cold water and let the rice return to a rolling boil. Check the rice to see if it's done. If not, repeat this process. Again, test the rice. If not done, repeat the process. Once done, drain the rice in a colander and immediately flush it with cold water. (This entire process will ensure that the rice is light, fluffy, and not sticky.) Place the drained rice into a pan and add 2 tablespoons of ghee. Place the ½ teaspoon of saffron threads in the palm of your hand and crush them with your opposite thumb. Add this to the rice. Gently toss the rice to cover it with the saffron. When you are ready to serve the rice, toss it again to disperse the colored grains.

Saag Paneer

Serves 4

Ingredients

For Paneer:

- 1½ quarts (6 cups) whole milk
- 3 tablespoons fresh lemon juice

For Saag: *(Spiced Spinach)*

- 3 cloves garlic, peeled and coarsely chopped
- 1 fresh hot green chili, seeded
- 1-inch piece fresh ginger, peeled and chopped
- ¼ cup whey (obtained from milk while making paneer)
- 4 tablespoons ghee, or sunflower oil
- 1½ teaspoons coriander
- ½ teaspoon cumin
- ¼ teaspoon garam masala
- ⅛ teaspoon cayenne
- ¾ teaspoon sea salt
- ¼ cup heavy cream (or half-and-half if you prefer something a little less rich)
- 2 10-ounce packages frozen, chopped spinach, defrosted (or 2 pounds fresh spinach)

Instructions

Pour the 1½ quarts (6 cups) whole milk into a large heavy saucepan and place on high heat. Bring to a boil, uncovered, stirring constantly to prevent milk from sticking to bottom of pan and burning. Watch closely; as soon as the milk begins to boil it will move quickly up the insides of the pan and may foam over the pot. As soon as it climbs upward, turn off the heat and add the lemon juice.

At this point the milk solids (curds) will separate from the liquid (whey). It will take about 10–12 minutes for 6 cups of milk to come to a boil, and another minute for curds to separate from whey. If not fully separate (the liquid should be clear), sparingly add a little more lemon until it does fully separate.

Drain curdled milk through a sieve or through layers of cheesecloth. Let sit for about ½ hour. Save whey (liquid) to use later in recipe. After ½ hour, remove from the colander and cut into ½-inch cubes.

Another version is to take the formed paneer and knead it until it is homogenous and smooth. Then, roll it into about ½- to ¾-inch balls and fry in ghee, or sunflower oil, until evenly golden. This occurs very quickly. Do not brown. Remove from the oil and drain on layers of paper towel.

In a blender or food processor, place 3 cloves chopped garlic, 1 seeded green chile, and 1 inch peeled and chopped ginger, along with ¼ cup whey. Blend. Add 1½ teaspoons coriander, ½ teaspoon cumin, ¼ teaspoon garam masala, ⅛ teaspoon cayenne, and ¼ teaspoon of sea salt. Blend again until thoroughly mixed. Pour into a small bowl and set aside.

In a large saucepan over medium heat, warm 4 tablespoons of sunflower oil or ghee. Add the spice mixture from the blender or food processor. (Careful, it can splatter.) Sauté spices, stirring constantly, for about 30 seconds.

Add spinach and ½ teaspoon sea salt. Stir gently for about 1 minute. Reduce heat to low, cover saucepan and simmer for about 7 minutes (15 minutes if using fresh spinach), stirring occasionally. Add a little whey if spinach begins to stick to bottom of saucepan.

Add ¼ cup cream to spinach blend and mix well. Puree spinach and cream in a food processor if a smoother, creamier spinach is desired. Place spinach back into saucepan if it has been pureed. Add the paneer pieces to the spinach mixture. Stir in ¾ cup whey. Bring to a simmer over medium heat, stirring gently. Reduce heat to low. Cover saucepan, and continue cooking for another 5 minutes, stirring constantly. Serve hot with basmati rice (see Saffron Rice with Ghee recipe above).

Tip: Paneer can be made ahead of time and stored in the refrigerator for up to two weeks. Store submerged in water. Change water daily. Pat dry before serving. Paneer also freezes well.

Vegetable Curry

Serves 3

Ingredients

- 3 cups vegetables (any combination you like)
- ½ cup frozen peas
- 2 tablespoons ghee, or sunflower oil
- ½ teaspoon cumin
- 1 teaspoon coriander powder
- ½ teaspoon turmeric
- 1 teaspoon sea salt
- ¼ teaspoon cayenne, or to taste
- ½ teaspoon anise seed
- 1 medium yellow onion, finely chopped
- ½ cup tomato, peeled and diced
- 1 tablespoon fresh lemon juice

Instructions

Peel and cut vegetables into ½- to ¾-inch pieces. If using root vegetables (e.g., carrots, parsnips, turnips, beets, potatoes), steam together in a steamer basket until crisp but still tender. Separately steam other "lighter" vegetables (e.g., broccoli, cabbage, cauliflower; the exception is frozen peas, which are defrosted and added during the last 2–3 minutes to prevent discoloration).

Do not overcook vegetables (see tip below). Warm 2 tablespoons ghee in a large skillet on medium heat. Add ½ teaspoon cumin, 1 teaspoon coriander powder, ½ teaspoon turmeric, ¼ teaspoon cayenne (or to taste), 1 teaspoon sea salt, and ½ teaspoon anise seed. Lightly sauté but do not burn the spices. (Ghee gets very hot quickly.)

Add 1 chopped onion and sauté until almost translucent. Add ½ cup diced tomato and cook for 5 minutes. Add the vegetables and cook for about 7 minutes. If desired, add a little water to thin the sauce.

Tip: This dish can be made ahead of time. If you are going to reheat, make sure the vegetables are steamed to about 90 percent of being done. That way when you reheat they will not be overcooked. Also, add the defrosted peas during the last 2 minutes of reheating the dish.

Mango Papaya Chutney

Approximately 3 cups

Ingredients

- 2 cups chopped, dried tropical fruits such as mango, papaya, or pineapple (unsulfured and unsweetened). A blend of these 3 is best.
- 1 cup hot water
- 2 tablespoons peeled and grated ginger
- 2½ tablespoons lemon juice
- ½ teaspoon cayenne, or to taste
- 1 teaspoon sea salt
- More water as needed

Instructions

Cover 2 cups tropical fruit pieces in 1 cup hot water, and set aside for ½ hour. (Alternatively, if in a hurry, cook for a few minutes until dry fruit softens.)

Combine softened fruit (with water they have soaked or cooked in), 2 tablespoons grated ginger, 2½ tablespoons lemon juice, ½ teaspoon cayenne, and 1 teaspoon sea salt in a blender or food processor.

Puree, adding more water as needed to form a thick, pudding-like consistency; or, if you prefer, leave it a little chunky. Allow to stand for a few minutes. Serve or refrigerate.

Variation: In this recipe, mango, papaya, and pineapple are used. But any combination of dried tropical fruits can be substituted.

Raita

Serves 6 generously

Ingredients

- 2 green cucumbers
- 1 teaspoon sea salt
- 2 tablespoons green onion, finely chopped (use white and green parts)
- 1½ cups low-fat yogurt, beaten with a fork until smooth
- 2–3 tablespoons lemon juice, or to taste
- ½ teaspoon cumin seeds
- 1 tablespoon chopped cilantro, or mint

Instructions

Peel cucumbers, halve them lengthwise and remove seeds. Dice one cucumber, and grate the other cucumber. Sprinkle with sea salt and let sit for 15 minutes. (This removes any bitterness.)

Rinse the cucumbers quickly in cold water. Drain well. Combine cucumber with 2 tablespoons chopped green onion, 1½ cups yogurt, and lemon juice to taste. Add sea salt if needed.

Heat a small skillet on medium heat. Lightly toast cumin seeds in a dry skillet, shaking the pan or stirring constantly. Bruise or crush seeds with a rolling pin and sprinkle over yogurt mixture. Serve chilled, garnished with chopped cilantro, or mint.

Lassi

Makes 3–4 cups

Blend in a blender:

- 1 cup low-fat plain yogurt
- ⅓ cup sugar (or honey, or agave)
- 4 ice cubes or 5 tablespoons water
- 2 cups cold water
- ⅛ teaspoon cardamom (optional)
- A few drops of rosewater (optional)

Serve well chilled.

Tip: Cardamom and rosewater bear strong flavors. Adjust amounts to taste if making multiple batches.

Chai

Makes 1½ quarts

Ingredients

- 6 cups cold water
- 1¼ teaspoons peeled and grated fresh ginger
- 2-inch piece of cinnamon stick
- 4 whole cloves
- 10 whole cardamom pods, lightly crushed
- 4 whole black peppercorns
- 7 tea bags (or 7 teaspoons loose) of Earl Grey, Darjeeling, or English Breakfast
- 4 tablespoons white sugar, or to taste (or light colored honey).
- 1 cup whole milk

Instructions

Put 6 cups cold water in a 2-quart stainless steel saucepan. Bring water to a boil. Add 1¼ teaspoons ginger, a 2-inch cinnamon stick, 4 cloves, 10 cardamom pods, and 4 black peppercorns.

Cover and simmer over low heat for 15 minutes. Add tea bags. Cover saucepan and remove from heat. Let steep for 3–5 minutes. With a fine strainer, strain out spices and tea. Stir in sugar and milk. Serve hot.

Potato Pea Samosas

Makes 10 large samosas

Ingredients

- 1½ cups unbleached white flour or Pamela's gluten-free flour
- ¾ teaspoon sea salt
- 1½ tablespoons ghee
- 9 tablespoons warm water (8 tablespoons if using gluten-free flour)
- 2 tablespoons sunflower oil
- ½ teaspoon cumin seed
- 1 medium onion, diced small
- ½-inch piece fresh ginger, peeled and finely grated
- 1 teaspoon coriander powder
- ½ teaspoon turmeric
- ½ teaspoon cayenne pepper
- ½ teaspoon anise seed
- 1 teaspoon sea salt (optional)
- 2 medium red potatoes, peeled, steamed, and mashed
- A dash of water
- ½ cup petite green peas
- The juice of 1 lemon or 1 teaspoon mango powder
- 4 cups light oil or ghee

Tip: Pamela's gluten-free flour makes 6 samosas. (Be sure to buy Pamela's bread mix and flour blend, and not the pancake mix.)

Instructions

Pastry Sift 1½ cups flour and ¾ teaspoon sea salt into a bowl. Lightly rub 1½ tablespoons ghee between the palms of your hands so that all parts of the flour are mixed with the ghee. Add 9 tablespoons warm water and mix until Ingredients are combined and the dough comes away from the sides of the bowl. Add a little more water if necessary. Knead firmly for 1–2 minutes or until the dough is smooth and elastic. Cover with plastic wrap and set aside for 30 minutes while preparing the filling. This will allow the dough to become more elastic. (If in a rush, skip this part.)

Potato Filling Heat 2 tablespoons oil. Add ½ teaspoon cumin and fry until brown. Add 1 medium diced onion, grated ginger (from a ½-inch piece), 1 teaspoon coriander powder, ½ teaspoon turmeric, ½ teaspoon cayenne, ½ teaspoon anise seed, and 1 teaspoon sea salt. Sauté until onion is tender. Add a dash of water. Remove from heat.

Add 2 mashed potatoes, juice of 1 lemon or mango powder, and ½ teaspoon cayenne pepper. Mix thoroughly. Add and mix in ½ cup petite green peas and set aside.

Making the Samosas Take the prepared dough and divide it into 5 balls. (If using gluten-free flour, divide into 3 balls.) Take one of the balls and, with a rolling pin, flatten it out on a very lightly floured surface. (Cover with plastic any dough balls you are not working on.) Using all the dough of each ball to make a circular shape. Round out the circle with a knife if necessary. Cut the circle in half. Fill a cup with warm water to dip your finger in.

With a paring knife, make a series of small, shallow, surface cuts along half the length of the straight edge of the half circle facing toward you. Dip your finger into the water and run it along this cut edge. Fold the half circle in half, making a cone shape by matching up the backside of the uncut half with the edge of the cut half so that there is a quarter-inch overlap. Push these together, making sure the length of this "seam" is intact, including the point of the cone.

Fill the cone with the seasoned potato–pea filling, just short of the top, leaving enough room to close it up. Lay the cone on its side with the seam in the middle. With a paring knife, make a series of small, shallow, surface cuts along the inside of the bottom of the cone and, using your finger, moisten it with a little warm water. Pull the top portion of the cone over the filling to meet the bottom side and press firmly but carefully. Take a fork and gently press it along this edge.

Trim the edge so that it is about ⅓ inch and no more. Make sure you haven't broken the seal. You can assemble all of the samosas and then fry them, or you can start frying and assemble as you go.

Frying the Samosas You will need a wok or a similar Indian-style cooking pan. A pan supported above the flame to diffuse direct heat is best.

When the 4 cups oil are hot enough, add the samosa(s). (Flick a few drops of water into the oil. If it sizzles, it's ready.) Adding the samosas will immediately cool down the oil. At some point, depending on how many samosas are in the pan at a time, you will need to increase the heat. Watch them carefully. If you are doing a lot of samosas, you will need to keep readjusting the heat of the oil. The oil should be bubbling. Cooking and browning them very, very slowly creates the most tender and attractive samosas. When they are nicely browned and you can see some of the dough slightly bubbling, remove them with a slotted spoon and place them on a plate or a platter covered with about 3 sheets of paper towels. Once the paper towels are soaked in oil, repeat this process with fresh paper towels before serving or freezing. As they cool, the pastry wrappings will "bubble" a little more.

The samosas will stay warm for about 1 hour. As they continue to cool, the pastry coverings will soften. You can let them cool and freeze them if you'd like. When you want to use them, defrost overnight, and again briefly fry in oil. This will take 2–3 minutes. They will need to be watched very carefully so that they don't overcook or overbrown.

Tamarind Raisin Chutney

Makes 1½ cups

In a food processor, blend (to be served with samosas)

- ⅔ cup soaked raisins
- 1 hot green chili
- 2 tablespoons fresh cilantro leaves
- 1 tablespoon fresh mint
- ⅓ cup concentrated tamarind
- ¼ teaspoon cayenne pepper
- ½ teaspoon garam masala
- ¼ teaspoon chat masala or black salt
- ½ teaspoon sea salt

Variation 1: Using Whole Wheat Pastry Flour and Baking the Samosas

Use the same dough recipe but with whole wheat pastry flour instead of unbleached white flour. Let the dough sit for 30 minutes. It will make 6–7 samosas. Prepare the samosas as described in the recipe. With a brush, spread melted ghee generously on all sides of the samosas. Place in a nonstick baking pan.

Put into a preheated oven at 350° for 20 minutes. Remove, and again spread ghee lightly over all surfaces. Return to the oven for another 8 minutes. Remove and set onto a plate covered with paper towels. Cool for 5–10 minutes before eating. (This is a great alternative, although "not the same." The crust is delicate, more like a pie crust, while in traditional samosas the pastry and filling "merge" in flavor.)

Variation 2: Samosa Pie

Use two prepared pie shells, or make your own. To fill the pie shell, multiply the recipe of the filling by approximately 4. If the filling is too dry, add a little water. Cover the pie with a pastry shell and pinch the two shells together at the edge. Brush the top with ghee. Bake at 350° for about 1 hour.

Carrot Halva

This delicious dessert is time-consuming. Make it when you have time and would enjoy a meditative activity.

Makes 28 1-inch-square, ½-inch-thick pieces
(use a 9 x 7-inch platter)

Ingredients

- 1 quart whole milk
- 2 cups carrots, peeled and grated (approximately 3 medium carrots)
- ¼ cup cashew nuts, finely chopped
- 2 tablespoons ghee or butter
- ¼ teaspoon ground cardamom
- ½ teaspoon saffron threads
- ¼ cup honey (light colored—whipped clover works well) or white sugar

Instructions

Actual cooking time: 1 hour and 45 minutes. Begin by heating milk in a wide, shallow, nonstick pan until warm. Add the carrots and cook over medium heat, stirring frequently. After 15 minutes of stirring, lower heat to a steady simmer and continue cooking.

Prepare the cashews by melting the ghee or butter in a small pot, then stir-fry the cashews for a few minutes until they are golden. Continue to watch and stir the carrot mixture frequently, scraping up any solids from the sides and bottom of the pan.

After the milk and carrot mixture has been reduced to half its original volume (which takes about 45 minutes or more), add ¼ cup chopped cashews, ¼ teaspoon cardamom, ½ teaspoon saffron threads, and ¼ cup honey or sugar.

Continue to stir and cook the mixture to an almost solid consistency. This will take up to an hour. To facilitate evaporation of the liquid, stir with a rapid circular motion. When almost solid, transfer the halva to an oiled platter and spread it evenly, patting it with the back of the stirring spoon. Allow to cool to room temperature, then chill in a refrigerator for about 2 hours. The cooling and chilling will further solidify the halva to the point that you should be able to slice the dessert into pie-like wedges or small squares or diamonds. Serve in small portions: halva is quite rich.

Halva will keep in the refrigerator for a couple of weeks. Alternatively, it can be made ahead and frozen. Before serving, defrost for 15 minutes or until it reaches room temperature.

For Your Health: Use a variety of tastes

Indian cooking often includes a variety of tastes in any given meal: sweet, sour, salty, bitter, pungent, and astringent. Traditionally, it is said that including all six of these tastes makes for a balanced meal, and helps the body digest the food properly.

Bhojanam swādishtamastu!
(Bon appetit in Sanskrit)

Part 4: *Specials*

- Healthy Smoothies
- Healthy Drinks
- Healthy Teas
- Sprouts
- Digestive Herbal Blends
- Summer Salads
- Gourmet Pizza
- Yeasted Breads
- Quick Breads
- Turkish Baklava
- Gluten-Free Desserts

Healthy

SMOOTHIES

1 Hemp Date Smoothie

2 Hemp Date Coconut Smoothie

3 Whey Berry Smoothie

4 Green Breakfast Smoothie

5 Green Protein Juice

Smoothies are a quick and easy way to get a nutritious breakfast or to reenergize yourself during the day. A healthy smoothie drink should contain all the nutrients of a complete meal. Choose a good-quality protein powder that is easy to digest. If you are new to smoothies, it is best to start with a sweet one. Choose fruits you like, such as bananas, mangoes, strawberries, or pineapple. Gradually add one leafy green vegetable such as kale, chard, parsley, spinach, or dandelion. Rotate the greens that you use.

Experiment with different ingredients to create new smoothies you enjoy. Keep the blend simple. Don't mix too many ingredients.

Place all ingredients in a blender and blend until smooth.

Hemp Date Smoothie

Makes 3 cups

- 2 cups organic unsweetened soy milk
- 1 large banana
- 3–4 Medjool dates
- 2–4 tablespoons raw hemp protein powder*
- 2 tablespoons almond butter

* See glossary.

Hemp Date Coconut Smoothie

Makes 3 cups

2 cups organic unsweetened coconut milk
1 large banana
2–4 tablespoons raw hemp protein powder*
3 Medjool dates
½ cup walnuts (soak in hot water for 1 hour, and drain)

Whey Berry Smoothie

Makes 4 cups

1½ cups rice milk
1–2 tablespoons ground flax seeds
½ cup of natural whey protein isolate,* unflavored
1 large banana
3 tablespoons raw pumpkin seeds, soaked overnight
3 tablespoons raw sunflower seeds, soaked overnight
½ cup berries (optional)

Tip: If you don't want to drink the seeds, strain the berries before adding them.

Green Breakfast Smoothie

Makes 3 cups

1 banana
1 teaspoon kelp powder or dulse
½ cup blueberries
2 kale leaves, no stems
2 cups water

Tip: If you don't want to drink the seeds, strain the berries before adding them.

Green Protein Juice

Makes 1⅓ cups

1 apple
1 small beet
2 stalks celery
3 carrots
1 inch fresh ginger root
1 tablespoon spirulina powder or 2 teaspoons Green Magma*

Tip: Juice apple, beet, celery, carrot, and fresh ginger. Whisk spirulina powder or Green Magma into the juiced vegetables so that it blends smoothly.

* See glossary.

Healthy
DRINKS

1
Strawberry-Watermelon-Ginger Juice

2
Pomegranate-Lime Juice

3
Orange Juice with Almonds

4
Almond Milk with Dates

This is a cooling and refreshing drink on a hot day. Both watermelon and strawberries are great sources of vitamin C. The sweet flavor of watermelon is well balanced with the slightly bitter, sour, and sweet taste of strawberries. The ginger adds a little zest and helps stimulate digestion. You can also enjoy watermelon juice by itself.

Strawberry–Watermelon–Ginger Juice

Serves 5 ~ Juice ingredients in juicer.

Ingredients

½ medium watermelon
1 pint strawberries
1–1½ inches fresh ginger root

Pomegranate-Lime Juice

Makes 1 cup

Ingredients

1 cup pomegranate juice
2–3 teaspoons fresh lime juice

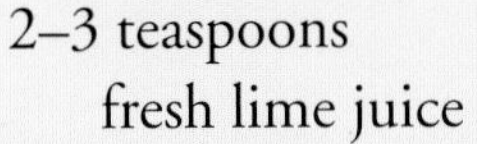

Pomegranates have lots of antioxidants, vitamins, and minerals, and are a powerful immune booster. If you can't find a fresh pomegranate, buy good quality, concentrated, 100 percent pomegranate juice. Dilute the juice with water if it is too sweet for you.

Stir the lime juice into a cup of pomegranate juice.

Orange Juice with Almonds

Serves 1 ~ Combine ingredients in blender and blend.

If you feel tired and/or weak and need a boost of energy, you can make a nut-citrus juice to uplift yourself. Almonds give strength to the body. Mixing almonds with orange juice, which is alkaline, is very refreshing and strengthening to the body. This drink gives physical strength and vitality. Paramhansa Yogananda highly recommended it.

Ingredients

12 raw almonds, soaked overnight and peeled
1 cup fresh orange juice (about 4 oranges)

Tip: Soaking almonds make them more digestible. In Ayurvedic medicine, almond skin is considered acidic and toxic to the liver. The almond skin is easily removed when the almonds have been soaked overnight.

Almond Milk with Dates

Makes 2 cups ~ Combine ingredients in blender and blend.

Ingredients

½ cup raw almonds (or soaked overnight)
1½ cups water
2–3 Medjool dates

This milk is a good and healthy substitute for cow's milk. Almonds are rich in dietary fiber, vitamins—especially vitamin B2—and antioxidants, and have one of the highest nutrient levels of all nuts. Almond drink by itself is a bit bland. Medjool dates are moist, juicy, and add a nice sweet flavor. You can also add other flavors, like carob powder, if you'd like.

Place ½ cup raw almonds and 1½ cups water in a blender and blend until smooth. Strain through a fine sieve, cheesecloth, or a nylon mesh bag used for sprouts.

Tip: Ratio of water to almonds can be 2:1 or 3:1.

Great Summer Thirst-Quenchers

Honey Lime Water
Makes 1 cup

Ingredients
1 cup water
½ teaspoon fresh lime juice
½ teaspoon honey

This drink helps calm the nervous system. Paramhansa Yogananda highly recommended it.

Mix and drink

Honey Lemonade
Makes 1 pitcher containing 5 ½ cups

Instructions & Ingredients

Mix together until dissolved:
1 cup boiling water
¼ cup honey

Mix in a pitcher:
Honey-water mixture
4 cups cold water
½ cup fresh lemon juice
(about 2–3 lemons)

Add 1 orange, thinly sliced. Refrigerate for 1–2 hours. Remove orange slices before serving.

Healthy
TEAS

Herbal teas help calm the body: drinking herbal tea is a good way to absorb the healing powers of herbs. These drinks are simple to make, and provide us with natural, effective herbal defenses against disease.

Nettle Tea

Nettle tea helps to build your energy, balance your moods, and support your respiratory system. Drinking nettle tea in the morning on an empty stomach helps to overcome an allergic reaction to pollen. You can buy dried nettle in the bulk section of a health food store, or order it online.

½ teaspoon of dried nettle

Put the tea in a tea infuser. Place tea infuser in 1 cup of hot water. Let steep for 3–5 minutes.

Lemon Balm Tea

Lemon balm helps to relieve tension, and is a good tonic for the nervous system. It is also a cleansing tea; so when you get a cold or flu, hot lemon balm tea will help you sweat out the toxins. You can grow lemon balm in your garden, buy dried lemon balm in the bulk section of a health food store, or order it online.

½ teaspoon dried lemon balm

Put the tea in a tea infuser. Place tea infuser in 1 cup of hot water. Let steep for 3–5 minutes. Remove tea infuser and drink. If using fresh lemon balm, add one or two lemon balm sprigs into a cup of hot water, let steep for about 5 minutes, remove sprigs and drink.

Fenugreek–Licorice Tea

Fenugreek contains enzymes that help digest plant protein. If you have a hard time digesting and assimilating plant protein, try fenugreek tea. You can blend fenugreek with licorice, which also aids digestion.

2 cups water • ½ teaspoon fenugreek
½ teaspoon chopped licorice root

Place ingredients into a small pot. Bring to a boil, turn off heat, and let steep for 10 minutes.

Digestive Tea

Makes ½ gallon (8 cups)

This simple tea can be drunk after a meal or between meals, to aid digestion; it includes three digestive seeds: cumin, coriander, and fennel.

8 cups water • ½ teaspoon cumin seeds
½ teaspoon coriander seeds • ½ teaspoon fennel seeds

Place ingredients in a pot and bring to a boil. Turn off heat, cover, and let steep for 20 minutes, then strain. Let the tea cool, then refrigerate. This tea can be drunk hot or at room temperature.

Teas for Each Season

Here are simple teas using herbs and spices that are in alignment with the energetic nature of each season.

To make 1 cup of tea, place ⅓ teaspoon of each ingredient (exception: use only a pinch of cloves) into a cup of hot water. Let steep for 5 minutes. Strain and drink after meals.

Summer	Fall & Winter	Spring
cumin	cumin	ginger
coriander	coriander	cinnamon
fennel	ginger	pinch of cloves

Fresh Herbal Tea

Makes 4 cups

You can grow herbs in your garden for fresh herbal teas. Easy herbs to grow are sage, mint, lemon verbena, and lemongrass • Sage is an aromatic shrub, considered to be an herb of wisdom and longevity. Its Latin name is "salveo," which means "to heal." It helps tone the body and is rich in antioxidants • Mint is a refreshing and cooling herb • Lemon verbena is an aromatic shrub that helps digestion • Lemongrass is an aromatic herb that helps to harmonize other flavors. It has vitamin C and a gentle taste of lemon, which adds zest to the mix.

To make a delicious, harmonious blend of these fresh herbs, boil 4 cups of water, turn heat off and add ingredients. Cover pot and let steep for 20 minutes. Strain and drink.

4 leaves of sage • 4 mint leaves (keep leaves on the stem) • 6 leaves of lemon verbena (keep the leaves on the stem) • 4 pieces (3 inches each) of lemongrass

Sweet Calming Tea

A blend of spices and honey.

Makes 4 cups

Mix ingredients in a pot. Bring to a boil, turn heat off, and steep for 10-30 minutes. The longer it steeps, the richer the flavor. Strain and add 2 teaspoons honey.

4 cups water • 3 cinnamon sticks • 2 pinches of saffron threads • 1 tablespoon cardamom pods

Masala Tea, Indian Style

Makes 2 cups

Bring to a boil:

2 cups water • 1 tablespoon fresh ginger root, grated • 1 tablespoon cardamom pods

Simmer for 5 minutes (or until water is reduced to about 1 cup). Add:

1 tea bag black tea • 1 cup warm milk

Turn heat off and let sit covered for 5 minutes. Strain and drink. Add honey/sweetener if needed.

Sprouts

Sprouts are a super-nutritious food and one of the most concentrated natural sources of vitamins, minerals, and proteins. They contain little or no fat! Sprouts have been grown and eaten for over five thousand years.

Sprouts are easy to grow in the kitchen all year around. Sprouting is easier than planting a garden. A few minutes of care a day and the sprouts (depending on the variety) are ready in three to seven days.

All that is needed is a little time and effort, and some water. The cost of sprout seeds is minimal. You can sprout seeds, beans, grains, and nuts. Some of the most popular sprouting varieties are alfalfa, broccoli, red clover, radish, mung beans, lentils, garbanzo beans, and peas.

The main benefit of sprouting is that it takes a seed or nut in its dormant state and brings it to life. During the sprouting process the nutrient value of the vitamins multiplies, and higher-quality proteins and other nutrients are produced.

In addition to the significantly higher nutritional value of sprouts, they are readily digestible. Because sprouts are living, growing food sources, they have a rich supply of enzymes. These proteins make sprouts easy to assimilate and metabolize. Sprouts are a powerhouse of nutrition and are in a form your body can easily utilize.

Sprouts can be used in salads and sandwiches, or added to soups, or stir-fried with vegetables. They also make a wonderful snack. You can eat them raw or cooked.

Sprouting is great fun, especially for children. They will love tracking the progress of their "sprouting farms." It's a great way to help them enjoy healthy food! You can buy a sprouting kit in a health food store. These kits make sprouting easier, but are not essential.

Sprouting Methods

In a Bowl

Soak 1½ teaspoons seeds or ⅓ cup beans in water for 8 hours or overnight.

Rinse and spread on the bottom surface of a strainer. Set strainer over a bowl deep enough that it does not touch the bottom, and cover the bowl with a bamboo mat or a breathable cloth.

Remove strainer and lightly rinse seeds or beans twice a day in fresh water. In 3 to 5 days, the seeds or beans will have sprouted and will be ready to eat.

In a Jar

Soak 1–2 tablespoons seeds or ¼ cup beans in water for 8 hours or overnight.

Rinse well and place in a Mason jar or other quart jar. Use either a screen lid, or a cheesecloth held by a rubber band, to cover the jar top. Lean the jar at an angle to allow the remaining water to drain from seeds or beans. (The goal is to keep the seeds or beans moist, not wet. If they stay wet, they will rot.) Rinse with water twice daily at regular intervals (e.g., 8 a.m. and 8 p.m.), draining each time.

Using a Sprouting Kit

There are various kinds of sprouting kits. Most are similar in how they are used: follow the directions specific to your own. These kits can make lots of sprouts at once, and may include up to 4 sprouting trays. Usually you will need to water the seeds or beans twice a day at regular intervals.

Over a few days the wet seeds or beans will expand to about four times their initial volume.

Don't put sprouting trays in direct sun. Most seeds and beans germinate best at room temperature, away from direct sunlight. Depending upon the temperature and the type of seed or bean, most sprouts will be edible in 3 to 5 days. Once seeds or beans are sprouted, take them from the trays and rinse them. Place in a container and refrigerate until you use them.

While kept in the refrigerator, rinse them every 3 days to keep them fresh and to prevent rotting. They will last for about a week.

Serving Suggestions for Sprouts

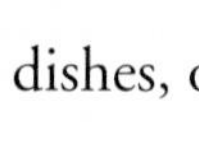

- Mix sprouts with jicama and a squeeze of orange juice and lime juice.
- Mix sprouts with green salad, cucumber, tomato, and salad dressing.
- Mix French green lentil sprouts with shaved carrot, add extra-virgin olive oil and Bragg's Liquid Aminos.
- Place sprouted black-eyed peas in a pot with water, bring to a boil and simmer for about 10 minutes. Mix the cooked sprouted beans with cooked brown rice.
- Drizzle a little Bragg's Liquid Aminos and extra-virgin olive oil over your sprouts, and add steamed broccoli or other vegetables for a complete meal.
- Add to breads, cereals, casseroles, soups, omelets, Oriental dishes, or cooked grains.

When Are the Seeds Ready?

- Seed sprouts, like alfalfa or red clover, are 1 to 2 inches long when ready.
- Bean sprouts, like lentils or peas, are ¼ to ½ inch long when ready, more tender when small.
- Mung beans are 1 to 2 inches long when ready. They are best grown in the dark to prevent bitterness. They should be rinsed 3 to 4 times a day. Taste the sprouts as they are growing to see when you like them best.
- Your indoor garden will grow best when the temperature is between 65° and 75° Fahrenheit.

Digestive Herbal Blends

Here are mixtures of herbs to help digestion, according to the season. Mix the herbs together and place them in a glass shaker. Label the container. Sprinkle on your food (salads, grains, beans, vegetable dishes, and soups).*

*Mix the herbs according to the proportions or ratios listed above. Depending on your need, the number "1" might represent one teaspoon, one tablespoon, or one cup. Whichever measure you use will be applied in proportion to every other ingredient in the recipe. If for example, you measure in teaspoons, the Fall-Winter recipe would be: 2 teaspoons of black pepper, 3 teaspoons of basil, 1 teaspoon of salt, 2 teaspoons of ginger, and 1 teaspoon of fennel, etc.

Summer	Fall & Winter
1 basil	2 black pepper
1 coriander	3 basil
1 sage	1 salt
3 fennel	2 ginger
2 turmeric	1 fennel
2 cardamom	
2 cumin	

Spring

1/2 black pepper	1 cumin
2 basil	1 mustard
1 cardamom	2 turmeric
1/4 cayenne	3 ginger

Summer

SALADS

Watercress Salad

Serves 3

Watercress is a spicy and stimulating herb that helps clear toxins and aid digestion. It has a cooling and refreshing quality.

Ingredients

3 tablespoons extra-virgin olive oil
2 teaspoons lemon juice
1 teaspoon honey
1 bunch of watercress leaves (about 2 cups, packed)
1 orange, peeled and divided into segments
Sea salt, to taste

Instructions

Place 3 tablespoons extra-virgin olive oil, 2 teaspoons lemon juice, and 1 teaspoon honey in a glass jar and shake to mix.

In a bowl mix the 2 cups of watercress leaves with the orange segments. Pour the dressing on top of the salad. Add sea salt to taste.

Tip: For milder flavor, use 1 cup watercress and 1 cup mild lettuce (such as butterhead), torn into bite-sized pieces.

Jicama Salad

Serves 4

Ingredients

3 cups jicama, peeled and cut into julienne (about ½ of a medium jicama)
1 medium carrot, peeled and grated (about ½ cup)
½ cup fresh orange juice
2 tablespoons fresh lime juice
1 teaspoon honey
¼ cup minced fresh cilantro

Jicama is a sweet root vegetable, a source of vitamin C, fiber, iron, calcium, and potassium. It can be eaten raw or cooked; during the summer it is juicy and refreshing eaten raw.

Instructions

In a bowl mix 3 cups julienned jicama and ½ cup grated carrot. In a small bowl whisk ½ cup fresh orange juice, 2 tablespoons fresh lime juice, and 1 teaspoon honey. Add to jicama mix. Garnish salad with ¼ cup fresh minced cilantro.

Alternative Recipe

Serves 4

Ingredients

2 cups jicama, peeled and grated
¼ red bell pepper, cut in cubes or small julienne
¼ cup fresh cilantro, coarsely chopped
zest (scrape off the outer surface of) ¼ lime
¼ cup lime juice (or equal parts lime and lemon)
2 teaspoons honey
1 pinch chili powder (if desired)

Instructions

Mix 2 cups jicama with ¼ cut red bell pepper, ¼ cup chopped cilantro, and the zest of ¼ lime. Mix ¼ cup lime juice with 2 teaspoons honey, and add to salad. If desired add 1 pinch of chili powder.

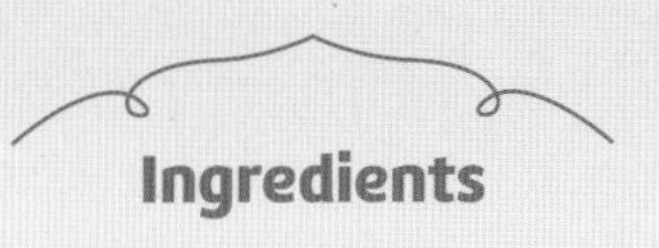

Ingredients

Lentil Corn Salad

Serves 4

1 cup dry red lentils, rinsed
3 cups fresh water
1 medium carrot, peeled and grated (about 1 cup)
¼ cup fresh lemon juice
1½ cups frozen corn, thawed
2 tablespoons organic, roasted tahini
2 tablespoons extra-virgin olive oil
1 teaspoon Bragg's Liquid Aminos, or tamari
¼ cup minced fresh parsley leaves
½ teaspoon sea salt, or to taste

This tasty summer salad is a quick and easy way to add more protein to your diet.

Instructions

In a pot, bring 1 cup dry red lentils (rinsed) and 3 cups fresh water to a boil.

Reduce heat to low and simmer with the lid slightly open for 10 minutes, until the lentils are soft but not mushy. Turn heat off, drain lentils, and set aside.

In a bowl mix together 1 cup grated carrot, 1½ cups thawed corn, and the drained lentils. Set aside.

Place in a blender ¼ cup fresh lemon juice, 2 tablespoons tahini, 2 tablespoons extra-virgin olive oil, 1 teaspoon Bragg's (or tamari), and ¼ cup fresh minced parsley leaves. Blend and pour over lentil mixture. Add ½ teaspoon sea salt, or to taste. Serve at room temperature. Garnish with minced parsley.

Summer Kamut Salad

Serves 6

This is a colorful, juicy salad to serve in the summer.

Ingredients

1 cup kamut,* rinsed
3 cups fresh water
¼ teaspoon Celtic salt
¼ cup extra-virgin olive oil
2 tablespoons fresh lemon juice
1 tablespoon Dijon mustard
½ teaspoon sea salt
⅛ teaspoon black pepper
1 medium raw beet, peeled and grated (about 1½ cups)
½ cup minced green onion (green and white parts)
1 medium orange, peeled and segmented
¼ cup minced cilantro

* See glossary.

Instructions

Overnight, soak 1 cup rinsed kamut in 3 cups fresh water. In the morning, place soaked kamut and soaking water in a pressure cooker. Add ¼ teaspoon Celtic salt.

Secure lid of pressure cooker and bring to a boil on high heat. Lower heat and simmer for 10 minutes (the time required will vary for different pressure cookers). Turn off heat. Set aside, letting pressure cooker cool down until it is safe to open.

In a small bowl whisk together ¼ cup extra-virgin olive oil, 2 tablespoons fresh lemon juice, 1 tablespoon Dijon mustard, ½ teaspoon sea salt, and ⅛ teaspoon black pepper. Set aside.

In a large bowl mix together cooked, drained kamut, 1½ cups grated beet, and ½ cup minced green onion (raw or sautéed in extra-virgin olive oil). Pour the dressing over the salad and toss to coat. Add 1 segmented orange.

Let sit at room temperature for 20 minutes to allow the kamut to absorb the flavors. Garnish with minced cilantro.

Gourmet
PIZZA

Gourmet Pizza

Makes one 12-inch round pizza

Ingredients

CRUST

0.25-ounce (1 small packet) baker's yeast
¼ teaspoon sugar or honey
¾ cup very warm water
1¾ cups unbleached white flour
¼ teaspoon sea salt

PIZZA SAUCE

¼ cup extra-virgin olive oil
½ onion, minced
4 or 5 cloves garlic, peeled and minced
¼ cup Burgundy wine
1 tablespoon sugar or honey
½ cup chopped fresh basil
6–8 ripe Roma or plum tomatoes, diced
¼ teaspoon black pepper
1 teaspoon dried basil
½ teaspoon dried rosemary
½ teaspoon dried oregano
1 small can tomato sauce, or tomato paste (thicker)

Selected Toppings

Mix and match items and amounts, according to your liking; use up to 4 or 5 items per pizza. Usually, ½ cup of each item is plenty for 1 pizza.

- Eggplant, peeled and sliced into ⅓-inch-thin, 1 x 2-inch pieces (marinate at least an hour ahead of time in 1 cup extra-virgin olive oil mixed with ¼ cup soy sauce)
- Red bell pepper, chopped
- Fresh spinach

- Fresh shiitake mushrooms, sliced
- Fresh garlic, minced
- Yellow onion, chopped
- Sliced green olives
- Sliced black olives
- Capers
- Marinated artichokes, sliced
- Mozzarella cheese, shredded
- Parmesan cheese, shredded
- Feta cheese, crumbled
- Blue cheese, crumbled
- Fresh basil
- Pesto sauce (available in most supermarkets, or make your own; as an alternative to tomato pizza sauce)

Instructions

CRUST Preheat oven to 500° or higher.

To make the crust, dissolve 0.25-ounce (1 small packet) baker's yeast and ¼ teaspoon white sugar in ¾ cup very warm water. Let rest for 8 minutes, or until yeast begins to activate (foam).

In a separate bowl combine 1¾ cups unbleached white flour and ½ teaspoon sea salt. Pour yeast mixture over flour mixture. Mix well. Turn dough onto floured surface and knead for 2 minutes. Form into a ball. For crispy thin crust, do not allow dough to rise—use immediately.

Oil a 12-inch round pizza pan (preferably the kind with holes in the bottom, to allow even baking) by lightly brushing the surface and sides with extra-virgin olive oil.

Spread the dough onto the base of the pizza pan. To prevent scorched edges, do not bring the dough too far up the side of the pan. With a fork, prick the surface of the dough to prevent "puffing" as it bakes.

PIZZA SAUCE

(Can be made the day before and refrigerated)

In a large saucepan warm ¼ cup extra-virgin olive oil on medium heat. Add ½ chopped onion and 4–5 cloves minced garlic. Sauté until transparent.

Add ¼ cup Burgundy wine, 1 tablespoon sugar or honey, ½ teaspoon black pepper, 1 teaspoon dried basil, ½ teaspoon dried rosemary, ½ teaspoon dried oregano, and ½ cup chopped fresh basil.

Add diced tomatoes. For a thicker sauce, add 1 small can tomato sauce or tomato paste. Adjust spices to suit your taste.

Cook over medium heat uncovered, stirring frequently, until sauce thickens (about 45 minutes). Remove from heat.

SELECTED TOPPINGS

Melanzane (marinated sliced eggplant) is a delicious pizza topping. Marinate eggplant pieces, an hour before, in 1 cup extra-virgin olive oil mixed with ¼ cup tamari or Bragg's Liquid Aminos.

Sauté selected toppings. (Sautéing allows flavors to deepen and the vegetables to soften.) Heat 6 tablespoons extra-virgin olive oil in a small skillet. Separately sauté until glossy, one topping at a time—e.g., chopped red bell pepper, spinach, sliced shiitake mushrooms, minced garlic, and minced yellow onion—placing sautéed toppings into separate small bowls.

Place other selected toppings into small bowls—e.g., sliced green olives, sliced black olives, capers, sliced marinated artichokes, shredded mozzarella cheese, shredded parmesan cheese, crumbled feta cheese, crumbled blue cheese, and fresh basil leaves.

ASSEMBLING THE PIZZA

Spread tomato pizza sauce (or pesto sauce, as an alter- native) thinly on uncooked pizza dough surface. Leave ½ inch at outer edge uncovered as a hand hold for pizza pieces. Sprinkle shredded parmesan cheese on edges. Sprinkle a layer of mozzarella cheese over the sauce.

- Add chosen toppings (see below for suggested combinations).
- Bake in 500° oven, or higher, for approximately 8 minutes, turning the pizza 180 degrees after 4 to 5 minutes so that it bakes evenly.
- Check the bottom for doneness by lightly lifting with a fork. (When fully cooked, the bottom of the pizza should be slightly golden brown.)
- Cut and serve.

Suggested Flavorful Combinations

Tomato sauce, mozzarella cheese, sautéed onion, marinated artichoke slices, sautéed red bell peppers, and feta cheese

Tomato sauce, mozzarella cheese, sautéed spinach, sautéed shiitake mushroom slices, and sautéed garlic

Pesto sauce, mozzarella cheese, sliced green olives, sliced black olives, and blue cheese

Pesto sauce, mozzarella cheese, marinated eggplant (melanzane), and capers

Yeasted
BREADS

1. Whole Wheat Bread, Rolls, Buns
2. Sesame Sticks
3. Carrot Pillows
4. Potato Bread

Here are basic techniques to use for the yeasted bread recipes that follow.

PREPARING THE YEAST MIXTURE

The temperature of the water is key: it needs to be lukewarm. It should not feel warmer than your wrist. Water that is too warm can kill the active dry yeast and prevent the bread from rising.

Measure into a small bowl the lukewarm water called for by the recipe. Add the active dry yeast and stir lightly to dissolve. Add sweetener.

Let stand until foamy (about 10 minutes).

PREPARING THE DOUGH

Mix other ingredients according to recipe. Fold active dry yeast mixture into other ingredients in a bowl. Stir until the dough holds together—it should be thick and moist.

Transfer the lump of dough to a clean, floured surface. Knead until smooth and elastic.

KNEADING THE DOUGH

If kneading by mixer: Use a mixer with a dough hook attachment, and let the dough knead for 10 minutes on low speed.

If kneading by hand: Fold the dough in, bringing the far edge toward you. Push down and forward, using the heels of the hands. Then turn the dough ¼ turn. Repeat the folding movement. Turn the dough ¼ turn again (turning always in the same direction). Continue to turn, fold, and push for about 10 minutes, until the dough is smooth, uniform, and non-sticky. Add flour if necessary.

THE RISING PROCESS

To prevent dryness, place the dough in an oiled bowl and turn it over so that the surface of the dough is oily. Cover the bowl with a damp towel or plastic wrap and put it in a warm place to rise. (It can take 30–90 minutes to rise, depending on the recipe.) The dough has risen when it has doubled its bulk. The time for rising will vary with the altitude, weather conditions, and temperature.

Take off the towel and "punch" down the dough (by pushing your fist steadily and firmly into it) 25–30 times all over. You can coat your fist with flour to prevent sticking.

Cut the dough into even pieces according to the recipe. Knead each piece 5–6 times and shape.

If using a baking tray: Oil the tray and place the shaped loaf on the tray. If baking more than one loaf on a tray, leave a 3–4–inch space between loaves. When baking rolls, leave a 1½–2–inch space between rolls.

If using a bread pan: Oil the pan and place the dough in the pan. Press the dough hard into the corners and floor of the pan. Take the dough out again and return it upside down to the pan. (This gives the bread a smooth-looking surface.)

Cover with a damp towel and let rise again (about 20 minutes).

BAKING THE BREAD

Brush the surface (see below).

Cut the top with ½-inch-deep slits to allow steam to escape (except in the case of rolls, where slits are not needed).

Sprinkle with seeds or herbs, according to the recipe.

Bake in preheated oven at 350°.

Remove from oven when the bread is done. To check whether the bread is done, note the color (according to the recipe and the type of surface brushing). Also, when you turn a loaf upside down and tap the bottom with your finger, the bread should resound with a deep, hollow thump.

BRUSHING THE SURFACE OF YEASTED BREADS AND ROLLS

There are four basic ways to coat the surface of yeasted breads and rolls:

1. *Egg Wash*: brush before baking with one egg beaten with 2 tablespoons water. Gives a golden-brown, shiny surface.
2. *Milk*: brush before baking. Gives a brown-colored surface.
3. *Ghee or Butter*: melt and brush before and after baking. Gives a soft surface.
4. *Water*: sprayed during baking gives a crisp, French-bread-type crust.

After coating the surface you can sprinkle sesame seeds (mix of tan and black), poppy seeds, sunflower seeds, pumpkin seeds, or rolled oats.

COOLING AND STORING THE BREAD

Remove from the pan or baking tray and let cool—ideally for 1 hour—before cutting and serving. Rolls can be served immediately after being taken out of the oven.

After the bread is completely cooled, it may be kept in a sealed plastic bag in the refrigerator, or frozen for later use.

Whole Wheat Bread

Makes 1 loaf or 12 rolls / buns

This is a basic whole wheat bread that is delicious and easy to make. The dough can be made into round loaves, braided loaves, buns, knots, or rolls, and it can be stuffed with vegetables and tofu.

Ingredients

- 2 cups lukewarm water
- 1½ teaspoons active dry yeast
- 1 teaspoon honey
- 3 cups whole wheat flour
- 2 cups unbleached white flour
- 1½ teaspoons sea salt
- 3 tablespoons sunflower oil
- 1 egg (for egg wash)

Instructions

Preheat oven to 350°. In a small bowl whisk 2 cups lukewarm water and 1½ teaspoons active dry yeast. Add 1 teaspoon honey and let it foam for 5–10 minutes.

In a large bowl mix 3 cups whole wheat flour, 2 cups unbleached white flour, 1½ teaspoons sea salt, and 3 tablespoons sunflower oil.

Fold foamed, active dry yeast mixture into flour mixture and mix thoroughly to create a dough. Knead and let rise (according to Instructions above) for 30 minutes or until dough has doubled in size. Then punch down and knead the dough again for 2 minutes.

Shape the dough (then cover it with plastic wrap or damp towel to prevent its drying out as it rises):

- **ROUND BREAD LOAF:** Shape into a round, place on an oiled 10 x 15-inch baking tray, and let rise for 20 minutes. Brush with egg wash and make slits (to allow steam to release).
- **ROLLS:** Divide the dough in half, and divide each half into 6 parts. Form into rounds and let rise. Then, brush with egg wash. You can incise an "X" on top of each roll with kitchen scissors.
- **BUNS:** Divide the dough in half, and divide each half into 6 parts. Roll each piece into a small ball and flatten. Let rise 5 minutes, then brush with egg wash and sprinkle with sesame seeds.
- **KNOTS:** Divide the dough in half, and divide each half into 6 parts. Roll each piece into a strand, then knot it and tuck in the ends. Let rise 5 minutes, then brush with egg wash and sprinkle with dried dill.
- **BRAIDED BREAD:** Prepare 3 strands and place on counter. Braid and shape into a long or a round braid. Cover again and let rise for no more than 20 minutes (or the dough will lose its elasticity). Then brush with egg wash and sprinkle on top a mixture of 3 parts tan sesame seeds and 1 part poppy seeds.

Bake for 20–40 minutes, or until the bread is golden brown. Let cool for 10–20 minutes before slicing.

Sesame Sticks

Makes 16 sticks

Ingredients

Whole Wheat Bread dough
2 tablespoons baking soda
2 cups cold water
1 cup sesame seeds (14 tablespoons tan, 2 tablespoons black)

Instructions

Start by making the basic Whole Wheat Bread dough (see previous recipe), let rise until doubled in size (about 30 minutes), then punch down. Preheat oven to 350°.

Divide the dough into 16 pieces. Cover them with a wet towel or plastic wrap. In a large, glass baking pan, dissolve 2 tablespoons baking soda in 2 cups cold water. In another flat pan, spread ½ cup sesame seeds.

Take each piece of dough and roll it into a rope (other shapes include a twist or a figure 8) about 6–8 inches long. Dip the strand into the baking soda solution, drain briefly on a kitchen towel, and roll in sesame seeds (add more sesame seeds if needed). Place on an oiled baking tray, leaving 1½ inches between sticks. Let rise 5 minutes.

Bake for 10–12 minutes or until golden brown. Cool briefly before serving. Sesame sticks are great dipped in extra-virgin olive oil and hyssop, or served with hummus dip and olives, or with soups and salads.

Carrot Pillows

Makes 16–22

Ingredients

3 cups water
1½ medium carrots, peeled and cut into chunks (about 1 cup)
½ cup lukewarm water
1 tablespoon active dry yeast
1 teaspoon honey
4 tablespoons extra-virgin olive oil
2 tablespoons water from cooked carrots (or plain water)
1 tablespoon honey
3½ cups unbleached white flour
1 teaspoon sea salt
1 egg (for egg wash)
Sesame and/or poppy seeds, or dried dill

Instructions

Preheat oven to 350°.

Bring 3 cups water to a boil. Add 1½ cut carrots, lower heat and simmer until carrots are soft (about 10 minutes). Drain and save water. Let carrots cool to room temperature for 10 minutes, then blend them in a blender or mash by hand.

While the carrots are cooling, mix ½ cup lukewarm water, 1 tablespoon active dry yeast, and 1 teaspoon honey in a small bowl. Let foam for 5–10 minutes.

In a large bowl mix 4 tablespoons extra-virgin olive oil, 1 cup cooked and mashed carrots, 2 tablespoons water from cooked carrots (or plain water), and 1 tablespoon honey. Add yeast mixture to carrot mixture. Combine ingredients thoroughly.

Place 3½ cups unbleached white flour and 1 teaspoon sea salt in an electric mixer. Add carrot/yeast mixture and combine, using the paddle. Add ¼ cup more flour if needed.

If kneading with the electric mixer, after mixing all ingredients change to bread hook and knead on low speed for 10 minutes. If kneading by hand, place dough on floured surface and knead for 10 minutes.

Place the dough in an oiled bowl, cover and let rise for 40 minutes. Punch down and roll the dough to ⅓-inch thickness. Cut into approximately 3-inch triangles, and place on an oiled baking tray. Leave about 1½-inch space between pillows (to allow them to expand and to keep the pillows from sticking to each other). Cover and let rise until doubled in size (about 15–20 minutes).

Brush with egg wash, sprinkle with sesame and/or poppy seeds, or dried dill weed (optional), and bake until golden (about 10–15 minutes).

Variations: Replace carrots with yams, winter squash, or potatoes.

Potato Bread

Makes one 12-inch round, flat bread

Ingredients

4 cups water
1 large russet potato, peeled and cut into ½-inch cubes
1 tablespoon active dry yeast
1 teaspoon honey
1 cup whole wheat flour
1¾ cups unbleached white flour
1 teaspoon sea salt
½ cup butter or ghee
3–4 sprigs of fresh rosemary
12-inch round pizza-baking pan

Instructions

Preheat oven to 350°. Place 1 cubed russet potato in 4 cups water and boil until soft, but not mushy. Strain and save water. Let cool to room temperature. Set aside.

In a small bowl prepare yeast mixture (1 cup lukewarm potato water, 1 tablespoon active dry yeast, and 1 teaspoon honey) and let foam for 10 minutes.

In a large bowl mash the cooked potato and combine with 1 cup whole wheat flour, 1¾ cups unbleached white flour, and 1 teaspoon sea salt. Add yeast mixture and combine thoroughly.

Knead for 10 minutes, then transfer dough into a well-buttered bowl and brush top with a generous amount of melted butter or ghee.

Cover and let rise 30 minutes, or until doubled. Punch down dough and roll to about ½-inch thickness (should be round and flat, like a pizza).

Place in an oiled 12-inch round pizza-baking pan. Make dimples on surface of dough with fingertips. Brush the top of dough again with melted butter or ghee, and let rise for about 20 minutes.

Sprinkle the top with fresh rosemary and bake for 20–25 minutes, or until golden brown. It should be light and fluffy.

Let cool and slice into wedges.

Quick BREADS

1 Pumpkin Bread

2 Zucchini Bread

3 Sesame Crackers

4 Ginger Cookies

Pumpkin Bread

Makes 1 loaf (9 x 5–inch glass loaf pan)

Pumpkin bread is a delicious quick bread. You can use it for a special breakfast or as an afternoon snack—and it's not too sweet.

Ingredients

- 1 cup canned pumpkin
- ¼ cup sunflower oil
- ½ cup maple syrup
- 1 teaspoon vanilla extract
- ½ teaspoon sea salt
- 1 teaspoon baking soda
- ½ teaspoon nutmeg
- 1 teaspoon cinnamon
- 1¾ cups whole wheat pastry flour

Instructions

Preheat oven to 350°.

In a large bowl mix 1 cup canned pumpkin, ¼ cup sunflower oil, ½ cup maple syrup, and 1 teaspoon vanilla extract.

In a separate bowl mix ½ teaspoon sea salt, 1 teaspoon baking soda, ½ teaspoon nutmeg, 1 teaspoon cinnamon, and 1¾ cups whole wheat pastry flour.

Mix dry ingredients into wet ones. Fold until just mixed (do not over-mix). Spoon and spread into oiled 9 x 5–inch loaf pan and bake for 40–50 minutes or until center is set and toothpick inserted into center comes out clean. (During baking, if the top starts to brown too quickly, cover with foil to keep it from burning.)

This bread freezes well: after it cools, wrap it in foil and place in freezer.

Variation: Replace the pumpkin with 1 cup mashed ripe bananas and ½ cup chopped walnuts.

Zucchini Bread

Makes 1 loaf (9 x 5–inch loaf pan)

A sweet and satisfying dessert. Can be served as an afternoon snack.

Ingredients

- 1 cup whole wheat pastry flour
- 1 teaspoon baking powder
- ½ teaspoon baking soda
- ½ teaspoon cinnamon
- ¼ teaspoon nutmeg
- ¼ teaspoon powdered ginger
- ⅛ teaspoon ground cloves
- ¼ teaspoon sea salt
- ⅓ cup sunflower oil
- 2 tablespoons fresh orange juice
- ½ cup maple syrup
- 2 eggs
- 1 cup grated zucchini (with or without peel)
- ⅓ cup raisins or unsweetened, shredded coconut
- ¼ cup chopped walnuts

Instructions

Preheat oven to 350°.

Mix and set aside 1 cup whole wheat pastry flour, 1 teaspoon baking powder, ½ teaspoon baking soda, ½ teaspoon cinnamon, ¼ teaspoon nutmeg, ¼ teaspoon powdered ginger, ⅛ teaspoon ground cloves, and ¼ teaspoon sea salt.

In a large bowl mix ⅓ cup sunflower oil, 2 tablespoons fresh orange juice, ½ cup maple syrup, 2 eggs, 1 cup grated zucchini, ⅓ cup raisins or shredded coconut, and ¼ cup chopped walnuts.

Mix dry ingredients into wet ones. Pour into well-oiled 9 x 5–inch loaf pan.

Bake for 40–50 minutes or until toothpick inserted into center comes out clean. (During baking, if the top starts to brown too quickly, cover with foil to keep from burning.)

Sesame Crackers

Makes 32 3 x 4 ¼-inch crackers

Ingredients

- 1¼ cups whole wheat flour
- 1 cup unbleached white flour
- 1 cup sesame seeds (use ¾ cup tan and ¼ cup black)
- 1 teaspoon sea salt
- 1 cup water
- 3 tablespoons sunflower oil
- 1 tablespoon Bragg's Liquid Aminos, or tamari

Instructions

Preheat oven to 400°.

In a large bowl mix 1¼ cups whole wheat flour, 1 cup unbleached white flour, 1 cup sesame seeds, and 1 teaspoon sea salt.

Add 1 cup water, 3 tablespoons oil, and 1 tablespoon Bragg's (or tamari).

Combine all ingredients until dough is created. Knead for 2–3 minutes.

Divide dough into two parts and place each half on an oiled, 12¾ x 17¾–inch baking sheet. Roll and press dough from the center to all sides. Roll with even pressure out to the edges so that you get an even thickness throughout the tray. (If the dough is not of a consistent thickness, the edges will burn while the center remains uncooked.)

Cut dough into 3 x 4¼–inch rectangles. Each tray will make 16 crackers.

Sprinkle lightly with sea salt (optional) and bake for 12–15 minutes or until golden brown. Store in airtight container and use as a snack for the next few days.

Gluten-Free Sesame Crackers

Same recipe as for Whole Wheat Sesame Crackers, but with substitutions for the first two ingredients.

- 1¼ cups organic brown rice flour (instead of 1¼ cups whole wheat flour)
- 1 cup garbanzo flour (instead of 1 cup unbleached white flour)

Follow the recipe just as for Sesame Crackers.

Ginger Cookies

Makes 36 cookies (using a 2-inch heart cookie-cutter)

Ingredients

1 cup room temperature butter, cut into small cubes
3 tablespoons molasses
½ cup maple syrup
3½ cups unbleached white flour
1 teaspoon cinnamon
2 teaspoons ginger powder
½ teaspoon nutmeg

In an electric mixer bowl, place 1 cup cubed butter, 3 tablespoons molasses, and ½ cup maple syrup. Mix on low speed until thoroughly combined.

In a separate bowl, mix 3½ cups unbleached white flour, 1 teaspoon cinnamon, 2 teaspoons ginger powder, and ½ teaspoon nutmeg. Add to wet ingredients. Dough will form.

Roll dough out on a countertop to ¼–inch thickness and cut with your favorite cookie cutter. Line cookie sheets with parchment paper and place ginger cookies ½ inch apart. Bake for 10–15 minutes. (To check whether done, lift edge of cookie with spatula. If the cookie bends, it's not done.)

Remove from oven and let cool. Cookies will harden as they cool.

Tip: If the dough gets crumbly, take one small piece at a time, and roll it into a small ball in the palm of your hand. Place the ball on the cookie sheet and press down with your fingers to flatten the ball and form a cookie.

Desserts

- *Turkish Baklava*

Gluten-Free Desserts:

- *Berry-Silken Tofu Mousse*
- *Coconut Whipped Cream*
- *Carob-Nut Balls*
- *Almond-Date Sweeties*
- *Maple Walnuts*
- *Coconut-Date Balls*
- *Lemon Tart*
- *Almond-Raisin-Chia Snack*

Turkish Baklava

12 x 18-inch baking pan (108 1 x 2-inch pieces)

Ingredients

1 cup water (skip this if using maple syrup)
2 cups white sugar (or xylitol or maple syrup)
1 teaspoon lemon juice (optional)
1 pound (16 ounces) raw, unsalted, shelled pistachios
1 box of filo dough (found in the frozen food section in most grocery stores), thawed a day ahead according to package Instructions
3 sticks (¾ pound) unsalted butter, or ghee

Instructions

(Skip this step if using maple syrup.) Bring to boil in a saucepan 1 cup water and 2 cups sugar (or xylitol). Allow to boil for a few minutes (stirring occasionally) until the mixture becomes syrup. Remove from heat. Set aside.

Using a food processor, grind 1 pound shelled pistachios into a slightly crunchy, mostly powdery form. Set aside.

Preheat oven to 350°. In a small saucepan, melt 3 sticks butter over low heat. Set aside. Unwrap thawed filo dough and unroll to full size. (Filo dough sometimes comes one package to a box and sometimes two smaller packages. If you get two packages, unroll each package and place the stacks side by side, the longer sides next to each other.)

Place a 12 x 18–inch baking pan (use only one that is sturdy) on top of filo sheet layers and cut filo to size of baking pan. Save "leftover" filo strips (edges beyond the 12 x 18 size). Grease the baking pan with a small portion of melted butter. Place about a quarter-depth of baking pan, of the stack of filo sheets.

Spread about ⅓ of the ground pistachios onto the filo. Repeat twice more, alternating layers of filo sheets and pistachio. Use leftover filo edge pieces on top of middle layers. Finish with last quarter of filo sheets on top.

Cut filo into 1 x 2–inch rectangular pieces or, preferably, into diamond shapes. (For diamond shapes, cut 1-inch-wide diagonal lines first, followed by 1-inch-wide straight lines parallel to the short edge of the pan.)

Pour melted butter over surface of filo, making sure to cover the entire surface.

Bake at 350° on middle rack of oven for about 25 minutes or until golden brown. Remove from oven. Pour syrup over evenly. Allow to cool before eating.

Tips:

- You may use a teaspoon of lemon juice in the syrup, which will prevent the sugar from crystallizing. Lemon juice is only needed if the baklava won't be eaten within a day or two.
- Use the filo soon after you remove it from its packaging, to prevent drying out and crumbling. If the filo comes out of the package crumbly, or with layers sticking to one another, it may have not thawed properly or it may be old filo that has thawed and been refrozen repeatedly. If it is too crumbly or sticky, you may have to use another package.
- Do not use disposable baking pans for baking baklava.

Serving Suggestions:

- Baklava tastes best the day after baking.
- Before serving, recut pieces, as the syrup tends to stick them together.
- Serve plain or with vanilla ice cream.
- Do not cover while still warm.
- Store leftover baklava at room temperature.

Gluten-Free Desserts

Berry–Silken Tofu Mousse

Serves 4–5

Ingredients

1 package sprouted silken tofu (12–14 ounces)
12 ounces fresh or frozen (and thawed) raspberries or blueberries
½ cup maple syrup
Whipping cream or Coconut Whipped Cream (see recipe below)

Instructions

In a food processor blend 1 package sprouted silken tofu, 12 ounces raspberries (save a few for décor), and ½ cup maple syrup until smooth.

Spoon mixture into 4–5 elegant cups, and refrigerate for 1–2 hours before serving.

Serve with whipping cream or Coconut Whipped Cream and more berries.

Coconut Whipped Cream

Serves 4–5

Ingredients

1 can organic full-fat coconut milk (18 grams total fat in a 13.5 oz. can), chilled overnight in fridge
2–3 teaspoons maple syrup
¼–½ teaspoon vanilla extract

Instructions

Chill 1 can of organic full-fat coconut milk overnight in the fridge (Chilling will separate the cream from the milk). Do not use light coconut milk.

Next morning, flip the can upside down. (The liquid coconut milk will rise to the top of the can.) Open can and pour coconut milk into a separate bowl. (You will not be using this part. Save the coconut milk for smoothies or soups.)

What will be left is the hardened coconut cream. Scoop this cream into a chilled bowl (place the bowl in a freezer for 5 minutes beforehand). Using a mixer, whip on high speed for 5–10 minutes until fluffy.

Add ¼–½ teaspoon vanilla extract and 2–3 teaspoons maple syrup. Whip again until stiff. Keep refrigerated until served.

Tip: Coconut whipping cream stiffens less than does regular (dairy) whipping cream.

Carob-Nut Balls

Makes 36 teaspoon-sized balls

Ingredients

- ½ cup honey
- ½ cup coconut oil (put container in warm water to liquefy)
- ½ teaspoon vanilla extract
- ¾ cup toasted carob powder
- ½ cup finely chopped walnuts
- ¼ plus ½ cup shredded, unsweetened coconut

Instructions

In an electric mixer cream ½ cup honey, ½ cup coconut oil, and ½ teaspoon vanilla extract. Transfer to a bowl. Add ¾ cup toasted carob powder, ½ cup finely chopped walnuts, and ¼ cup shredded, unsweetened coconut. Mix.

Make small balls and roll in shredded coconut to cover the outside surface.

Refrigerate for a few hours, or overnight, before serving. The balls will firm up as they chill.

Almond-Date Sweeties

Makes 27 small or 10 large diamond-shape sweeties

Ingredients

- 1 cup raw almonds
- 1 cup chopped Medjool dates
- 2 tablespoons water
- 2 dried pineapple rings, broken into small pieces
- 2 tablespoons liquefied coconut oil (put container in warm water to liquefy)
- ⅓ plus ½ cup unsweetened coconut flakes

Instructions

In a food processor, grind 1 cup raw almonds. Remove. Next place 1 cup chopped Medjool dates and 2 tablespoons water in the food processor and blend. Add dried pineapple pieces, 2 tablespoons liquefied coconut oil, and ⅓ cup unsweetened coconut flakes. Blend. The mixture should have a sticky consistency.

In a 7½ x 11½-inch glass pan, sprinkle a thin layer (about ¼ cup) of unsweetened coconut flakes and place mixture on top. Flatten it with the palm of your hand. Sprinkle with remaining ¼ cup unsweetened coconut flakes.

With a knife, cut into squares, diamonds, or rectangle shapes. Cover with plastic wrap and chill in the freezer for at least 2 hours, or overnight (until hardened). Then serve.

Maple Walnuts

Makes 4 cups

Ingredients

4 cups walnuts, soaked
¼ cup maple syrup
4 teaspoons ghee, melted
1 teaspoon cinnamon
1 teaspoon sea salt

Instructions

Optional: In a bowl soak 4 cups walnuts in water for 3 hours to eliminate any bitter aftertaste. If limited for time, soak walnuts in warm water for ½ hour. Rinse and pat dry with towel. Place soaked walnuts on baking tray, one layer thick, and bake at 200° for 20–30 minutes or until dry.

In a small bowl mix ¼ cup maple syrup, 4 teaspoons melted ghee, 1 teaspoon cinnamon, and 1 teaspoon sea salt. Place the dried walnuts in a large bowl, add maple mixture and coat well.

Put nuts in an oiled baking tray, one layer thick, and bake at 300° for 20 minutes. Walnuts should be crisp and delicious.

Tip: If making a big batch, use 20 cups walnuts, 1 cup maple syrup, ½ cup ghee, 4 teaspoons cinnamon, and 2 teaspoons sea salt.

Coconut-Date Balls

Makes 15 tablespoon-sized balls

Ingredients

½ cup walnuts
½ cup chopped Medjool dates
½ cup shredded, unsweetened coconut
¼ cup honey

Instructions

In a food processor, grind ½ cup walnuts until fine. Add ½ cup chopped Medjool dates, ½ cup shredded coconut, and ¼ cup honey.

Put mixture in a bowl and make into tablespoon-sized balls. Roll in shredded coconut.

Lemon Tart

Serves 6

Ingredients

½ cup coconut oil, melted
¼ cup Medjool dates, pitted
1–3 tablespoons water
1⅓ cups macadamia nuts, raw unsalted
Date paste
A pinch of sea salt
2 bananas
Zest of 1 lemon (Meyer lemon preferred)
4 tablespoons fresh lemon juice
2 tablespoons organic honey
½ teaspoon vanilla extract
½ cup melted coconut oil
Fresh berries or lemon zest

Instructions

Place ½ cup coconut oil in a small bowl. Place the small bowl in a larger one that has room to add water. Pour hot water into the larger bowl, being careful not to get water in the oil. Leave until the oil has melted. (If the water cools before the oil is completely melted, pour off cool water and add hot.)

To prepare the crust, put ¼ cup pitted Medjool dates and 1 tablespoon water in a food processor. Make a paste with the water and dates by first pulsing the processor several times to allow the dates to break down. Then continue to pulse until a smooth paste is achieved. If the dates are too dry, you will need to add more water, one tablespoon at a time.

Remove the paste from the processor bowl and set aside. Wipe the processor bowl (you do not have to clean it thoroughly).

Place 1⅓ cups macadamia nuts in the food processor and process nuts until they are medium-fine crumbs. Add the date paste and salt, and process until combined. It will form a ball in the processor bowl. (There is no need to process until smooth, as some texture in the crust is nice.)

Place equal amounts of the dough into 3 4-inch tart pans, or use one larger one. Smooth out the crust until it is somewhat flat on the bottom of the pan. Create a fluted edge by pinching the crust dough up the sides of the pan, smoothing out where necessary.

Using the food processor again, put in 2 bananas, the zest of 1 lemon, 4 tablespoons fresh lemon juice, 2 tablespoons organic honey, ½ teaspoon vanilla extract, and ½ cup melted coconut oil. Process until smooth and creamy.

Pour filling into the tart pans until they are full. Refrigerate until set (at least 3 hours). (For quicker setting, put tarts in the freezer for ½–1 hour, then remove and place in refrigerator.) Before serving, remove from fridge and let sit at room temperature for 30–60 minutes. To serve, remove from tart pan ring and place on a plate. Top with fresh berries or more lemon zest.

Variation: You can use any nuts, such as walnuts or almonds, but macadamia nuts are preferred.

Almond-Raisin-Chia Snack

Serves 1

An afternoon nondairy, gluten-free snack

Ingredients

- 1 cup unsweetened almond milk (vanilla flavor)
- 2 tablespoons raisins
- 2–3 pieces unsulfured dried apricot (optional)
- 2 tablespoons chia seeds*

* See glossary.

Instructions

Mix in a bowl: 1 cup unsweetened almond milk, 2 tablespoons raisins, 2–3 pieces unsulfured dried apricot (optional), and 2 tablespoons chia seeds.

Cover and let sit at room temperature for 4–6 hours before eating. This will allow the chia seeds to expand and create a more creamy consistency.

Make sweet desserts
for sweet friends

Part 5: *Basic Recipes*

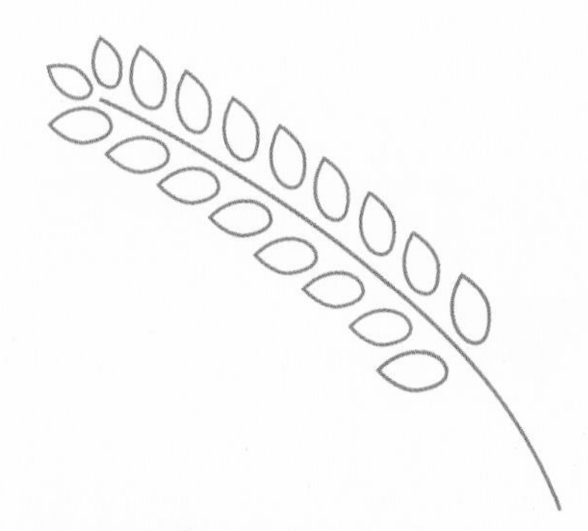

- Breakfast Cereals
- Grains
- Legumes
- Vegetables
- Sauces
- Dressings

Basic

RECIPES

These are samples of assorted simple recipes you can incorporate into your meals.

Breakfast Cereals

- Coconut Rice Cereal
- Amaranth Porridge with Apples
- Multigrain Cereal

Grains

- Herbed Millet Casserole
- Golden Rice Quinoa
- Sesame Brown Rice

Legumes

- Tofu and Tempeh
- Marinades for Tofu & Tempeh
- Tofu Salad
- Herbed Tofu
- Baked Tempeh Cubes
- Mung Bean Vegetable Soup
- Split Mung Coconut Soup
- Mung Dhal with Carrots
- Garbanzo Marinade

Vegetables

- Curried Brussels Sprouts
- Mashed Root Vegetables

Sauces

- Black Bean Sauce
- Mung Bean Coconut Sauce
- Zucchini-Carrot Sauce
- Green Sauce
- Orange-Cashew Sauce
- Orange-Ginger Sauce
- Lemon Herb Sauce

Dressings

- Tahini-Dill Dressing
- Tahini-Ginger Dressing
- Vitality Dressing
- Miso Dressing
- Lemon-Ginger Dressing

Breakfast Cereals

A breakfast of nourishing food is an important part of starting your day. When the weather is warm, you might enjoy smoothies, fruits, and nut butters. When the weather is cold, you can introduce warm cereals, soups, and grains such as rice, quinoa, and millet. Here are a few warm breakfast cereals.

Coconut Rice Cereal

Serves 3–4

Ingredients

3 cups water
A pinch of sea salt
⅔ cup jasmine rice, rinsed
⅓ cup amaranth, rinsed
¼ cup shredded coconut

Instructions

Place 3 cups of water in a pot with a pinch of sea salt. Add ⅔ cup jasmine rice, ⅓ cup amaranth (for protein and texture), and ¼ cup shredded coconut. Bring to a boil and simmer for about 15–20 minutes until all water is absorbed. Turn the heat off, cover, and let sit for 10 minutes. Fluff with a fork.

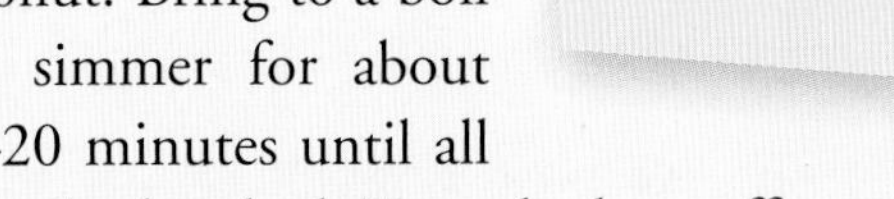

Serving Suggestion: Serve with honey, ghee, and raisins.

Amaranth Porridge with Apples

Serves 4

Ingredients

1 cup amaranth, soaked overnight
4 cups water
2 cups coconut milk, unsweetened
2 cups chopped apples
A pinch of sea salt

Instructions

Soak overnight 1 cup amaranth in 3 cups of water.

Next morning, drain water through a tight mesh sieve. In a medium-size pot put soaked amaranth, 1 cup of water, 2 cups unsweetened coconut milk, 2 cups chopped apples, and a pinch of sea salt. Mix all the ingredients.

Partially cover pot, bring to a boil, and simmer for 20 minutes, stirring occasionally. Turn heat off, cover pot fully, and let sit for 10 minutes.

Serving Suggestion: Serve with honey, chopped walnuts and dates, and yogurt.

Multigrain Cereal

Serves 3–4

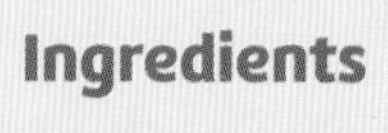

Ingredients

½ cup 7-grain or multigrain cereal (buy in bulk at a health food store)
½ cup steel-cut oats
(To cut cooking time in half, soak cereal and oats overnight, or soak for 1–2 hours in hot water, before cooking.)
3–4 cups water
A pinch of sea salt
½ cup chopped dates

Instructions

Mix together ½ cup 7-grain cereal and ½ cup steel-cut oats. Rinse. Place grains in a pot and add 3 to 4 cups of boiling water. Let sit for 2 hours.

Two hours later add a pinch of sea salt, and ½ cup chopped dates (optional). Bring to a boil. Leave the lid slightly open, and simmer for 10 minutes.

Variation: Soak grains with ½ cup less water, and when cooking, add ½ cup milk. This will make the cereal more creamy and rich.

Serving Suggestion: Serve with yogurt, roasted walnuts, and maple syrup.

Tip: A 7-grain mix includes such grains as buckwheat, barley, millet, yellow corn, and bulgur.

Grains

Herbed Millet Casserole

Serves 4–6

Ingredients

1 cup millet
2 teaspoons dried basil
2 teaspoons dried oregano
3 cups water
A pinch of sea salt
1 tablespoon sesame oil
1 tablespoon lemon juice
1½ cups cauliflower flowerets, cut into small pieces
½ cup diced carrot

Instructions

Preheat oven to 350°. Heat (over medium heat) a cast-iron skillet. Place 1 cup dry uncooked millet in the skillet, turning often with a spoon or a spatula until the millet is lightly browned. (Dry roasting adds aroma and flavor to the grain.)

In a bowl, mix dry roasted millet with 2 teaspoons basil and 2 teaspoons oregano. Place the millet mixture into a casserole dish. (Baking grains creates a nutty, soft, and fluffy texture.)

Add a pinch of sea salt to 3 cups boiling water, and add to the millet mixture. Add 1 tablespoon sesame oil, 1 tablespoon lemon juice, 1½ cups cut cauliflower flowerets, and ½ cup diced carrot. Cover with foil and lid to seal. Bake at 350° for 45–50 minutes.

Serving Suggestion: Serve with Black Bean Sauce (see page 243) or Green Sauce (see page 244). Garnish with parsley or cilantro.

Golden Rice Quinoa

Serves 4–6

Ingredients

¾ cup basmati rice, rinsed
¾ cup quinoa, rinsed
1½ tablespoons extra-virgin olive oil
½ teaspoon turmeric
3¼ cups water
½ teaspoon sea salt
Cilantro leaves

Instructions

Oil the bottom and sides of a rice cooker bowl. Mix together ¾ cup basmati rice and ¾ cup quinoa and place in the rice cooker. Fold in 1½ tablespoons extra-virgin olive oil, ½ teaspoon turmeric, 3¼ cups water, and ½ teaspoon sea salt.

Turn rice cooker on and cook until done. Remove cover and lightly fluff with a wooden spoon. Garnish with cilantro leaves.

Tips:

- A rice cooker is good for cooking the lighter grains such as white rice and quinoa. A mixture of white rice and quinoa has a pleasant texture and flavor.
- Turmeric adds a golden color, and is known to improve digestion.

Serving Suggestion: Serve with Green Sauce (see page 175), which helps moisten the grains.

Sesame Brown Rice

Serves 3–4

Ingredients

1 cup short grain brown rice (presoaked)
2 cups water
¼ teaspoon Celtic salt
3 tablespoons sesame seeds
1–2 tablespoons sesame oil
3 green onions, minced
1–2 tablespoons Bragg's Liquid Aminos, or tamari

Instructions

Put into a rice cooker: soaked short grain brown rice, 2 cups water, and ¼ teaspoon Celtic salt. Place cover on rice cooker and turn on.

While the rice is cooking, heat a cast-iron skillet over medium heat. When the skillet is hot, put in 3 tablespoons sesame seeds, stirring to dry roast until seeds turn a golden brown. Set roasted seeds aside.

In the same skillet place 1 to 2 tablespoons sesame oil and heat over medium heat. Add 3 green onions, minced. Sauté for 2 to 3 minutes. Add 1 to 2 tablespoons Bragg's (or tamari).

When the rice has finished cooking, remove lid of rice cooker, fluff rice, and place in a bowl. Add sesame seeds and green onions. Serve warm.

Legumes

Tofu and Tempeh

Tofu and tempeh are great sources of vegetarian protein. There are numerous, tasty soy- and tofu-based meat and dairy alternatives available if you are transitioning to a meatless diet. However, there is a lot of protein in legumes and grains also, so use soy products as a supplement to your diet, not the main focus. Tofu is a smooth soybean curd with a neutral taste.

Tempeh has a slightly nutty, earthy flavor and has the texture of soybeans.

The following are examples of tofu and tempeh that can be used in vegetarian meals.

Types of Tofu Tofu or bean curd is made by soaking, grinding, boiling, and straining mostly dried soybeans. Then the soy milk is coagulated and pressed into soft white blocks. Tofu is rich in iron, contains little fat, and has a low amount of calories. Depending on the coagulant used in processing, the tofu may also be high in magnesium and calcium. Tofu can be used in sweet dishes, but it is more often used in savory ones.

Firm or Extra-Firm Tofu This type of tofu is dense and solid and holds its shape. It has been drained and pressed but still contains a good amount of moisture. The texture of the inside of the tofu is similar to a firm custard. The pattern of the tofu skin takes the shape of the strainer used to drain it. Tofu is used in stir fry, soups, or baking. The firmer the tofu, the longer it will take to absorb flavor, and the tougher the tofu may become after cooking.

Silken (Soft) Tofu This type of tofu is creamy and custard-like. It is fresh tofu that has not been drained and therefore contains the highest moisture content. It is used in mostly pureed form, such as salad dressings, blended dishes, and desserts.

Types of Tempeh Tempeh is traditionally a soybean product. Natural culturing and fermentation bind whole soybeans into a cake that is easily digestible, has a firm texture and an earthy flavor. Because it uses the whole bean, tempeh is very nutritious, and retains the soybean's high protein, vitamin, and fiber content. Tempeh comes in many varieties, including ones mixed with different seasonings and foods (e.g., peanuts, coconut, fruit, and sugar), as well as ones made from different grains (e.g., barley and oats).

Cooking Techniques Tofu and tempeh are like sponges: They will absorb the flavor of the foods and spices with which they are mixed. See the recipes on the following pages for suggestions for different marinades.

Usually you can buy tofu or tempeh in a package of 14 ounces or 1 pound. One package typically Serves 3–4 people.

Cut tofu or tempeh into a variety of shapes, to fit the dish you are making. Serve with grains, vegetables, sauces, or salads.

Steaming Steam the tofu to make it more digestible.

- Place tofu in a steamer over boiling water and steam for 5–10 minutes.
- Place on a cutting board and cut into cubes, or place in a bowl and mash with a fork, or cut to the shape you want for a particular dish.

Sautéing

- Heat 2 tablespoons oil in a pan (sunflower oil works well).
- Sauté tofu or tempeh in a pan, on medium-high heat for 5 to 10 minutes, until golden.
- Sprinkle with seasonings.

Baking

- Slice the tofu or tempeh in half, then cut in flat rectangles, triangles, or cubes. In general, the firmer the tofu/tempeh, the smaller you can cut it.
- You can add flavor by mixing the marinade and tofu/tempeh pieces in a bowl first, or by pouring the marinade over them. Let it sit for an hour or so.
- Heat oven to 350°. Bake uncovered for about 20 to 30 minutes until golden. If using tempeh, toss and turn every 10 minutes for more even cooking.

Marinades for Tofu and Tempeh

Mix together and pour over tofu or tempeh:

Ginger–Garlic Marinade

Makes ⅔ cup

¼ cup Bragg's Liquid Aminos, or tamari
⅓ cup water
1 tablespoon sesame oil
1½ teaspoons fresh ginger root juice*
2 cloves garlic, peeled and minced

Sesame–Tamari Marinade

Makes 1 cup

⅓ cup fresh water
⅓ cup Bragg's Liquid Aminos, or tamari
2 tablespoons sesame oil
2 tablespoons sesame seeds

*See glossary on how to make ginger juice.

Salty Marinade

Makes ⅓ cup plus 1 tablespoon

2 tablespoons sesame oil
2 tablespoons Bragg's Liquid Aminos, or tamari
1 tablespoon fresh ginger root juice*
2 tablespoons water

Sweet-and-Salty Marinade

Makes ½ cup

¼ cup Bragg's Liquid Aminos, or tamari
1 tablespoon fresh lemon juice
1 tablespoon maple syrup
1 tablespoon sesame oil
1 tablespoon fresh ginger root juice*

* See glossary for how to make ginger juice.

Recipes

Tofu Salad

Serves 3–4

Ingredients

- 1 pound extra-firm tofu
- 3 tablespoons extra-virgin olive oil
- 3 tablespoons fresh lemon juice
- 3 tablespoons Bragg's Liquid Aminos, or tamari
- 1 medium carrot, peeled and minced
- 1 celery stalk, minced
- ½ cup sliced black olives

Instructions

Rinse the tofu, then place it in a steamer over boiling water and steam for 5 to 10 minutes. (This step is optional, but does make tofu more easily digestible.)

Separate the tofu into chunks with a knife or with your hands. Place the tofu cubes in a bowl and mash with a fork. Set aside.

In a small bowl whisk together 3 tablespoons extra-virgin olive oil, 3 tablespoons fresh lemon juice, and 3 tablespoons Bragg's (or tamari). Add the mixture to a bowl with mashed tofu and blend by hand.

Add 1 minced carrot, 1 minced celery stalk, and ½ cup of sliced black olives. Mix all the ingredients well. Refrigerate for 30 minutes to 2 hours before serving, to allow absorption of flavors.

Serving Suggestion: Serve with blue corn chips. This salad can also be used as a sandwich spread.

Herbed Tofu

Serves 3–4

Ingredients

1 pound extra-firm tofu
2 tablespoons sunflower oil
1–2 teaspoons garlic powder
1–2 teaspoons dried thyme (optional)
1–2 tablespoons nutritional yeast
1½ tablespoons Bragg's Liquid Aminos, or tamari
Fresh-squeezed juice of ½ lemon (optional)

Instructions

Drain and wrap 1 pound of tofu in a paper towel to absorb excess water. Cut tofu into 1-inch cubes.

Heat 2 tablespoons sunflower oil in a skillet on medium-high heat. Sauté tofu cubes with 1 to 2 teaspoons garlic powder for 5 minutes. Sprinkle over tofu cubes 1 to 2 teaspoons dried thyme (optional) and 1 to 2 tablespoons nutritional yeast.
Continue sautéing and stirring until tofu cubes are golden and crisp on the outside (about 10 minutes).
Turn heat off and add 1½ tablespoons (or to taste) of Bragg's or tamari. Squeeze in the juice of half a lemon (optional). Serve warm or cold.

Serving suggestions: Can be served as a snack, or as a main dish for lunch or dinner, accompanied by a green salad.

Baked Tempeh Cubes

Serves 3–4

Ingredients

1 pound tempeh, cut into 1-inch cubes
2 tablespoons extra-virgin olive oil
3 tablespoons lemon juice
1 tablespoon Bragg's Liquid Aminos, or tamari
2 tablespoons water

Instructions

Heat oven to 350°. To make marinade, whisk in a bowl 2 tablespoons extra-virgin olive oil, 3 tablespoons lemon juice, 1 tablespoon Bragg's Liquid Aminos (or tamari), and 2 tablespoons water. Put 1 pound cubed tempeh in a glass dish and pour the marinade over the cubes.

Bake uncovered for about 30 minutes, lightly turning cubes every 10 minutes. Bake until crisp and golden brown.

Tip: Marinating before baking infuses tempeh or tofu with flavor. You can marinate them for as little as 10 minutes and as long as overnight. The longer you marinate tempeh or tofu, the more flavorful the dish will be.

Mung Bean Vegetable Soup

Serves 4–6

Ingredients

2–3 tablespoons sunflower or sesame oil
1 cup minced yellow onion
½ cup minced turnip
1½ cups minced green cabbage
A pinch of Celtic salt
7 cups water
2 tablespoons vegetable broth powder
1 cup split mung beans, rinsed
1½ cups yam, peeled and cut into 1-inch cubes
3 cups chopped kale leaves (without stems)
1½ teaspoons sea salt
Bragg's Liquid Aminos, to taste

Instructions

Heat 2–3 tablespoons sunflower or sesame oil in a pressure cooker. When the oil has heated, add 1 cup minced yellow onion. Sauté lightly.

Add ½ cup minced turnip, 1½ cups minced green cabbage, and a pinch of Celtic salt.

Add 1 cup split mung beans and 7 cups water. (Split mung beans absorb water. Not adding enough water will create an overly thick consistency.)

Add 2 tablespoons vegetable broth powder, ½ cup cubed yam, and 3 cups chopped kale.

Secure lid of pressure cooker and turn to high heat. When the pressure cooker comes to full steam, lower the heat and simmer for 10 minutes (the time required will vary for different pressure cookers).

Turn off heat. Let the pressure cooker cool down until it is safe to open. Remove lid and add 1½ teaspoons sea salt and Bragg's Liquid Aminos, to taste.

Tip: To make a creamier soup, pour part of the slightly cooled soup into a blender and blend, then add to the remaining soup.

Serving Suggestion: Serve with whole wheat tortillas, or cooked grains, or bread.

Split Mung Coconut Soup

Makes 4 ½ cups. Serves 2–3.

Ingredients

2 tablespoons coconut oil
1 cup minced onion
A pinch of Celtic salt
1 medium carrot, peeled and chopped
2 cups water
2 cups coconut milk
2 tablespoons vegetable broth powder
¾ cup split mung beans, rinsed
¼ teaspoon dried dill, or ¾ teaspoon fresh dill (optional)

Instructions

Heat 2 tablespoons coconut oil in a pressure cooker. When the oil has heated, add 1 cup minced onion and a pinch of Celtic salt. Sauté onion until golden. Add 1 chopped carrot, 2 cups water, and 2 cups coconut milk. Mix in 2 tablespoons vegetable broth powder and ¾ cup split mung beans.

Secure lid of pressure cooker and turn to high heat. When the pressure cooker comes to full steam, lower heat and simmer for 5 minutes (the time required will vary for different pressure cookers). Turn off heat. Let pressure cooker cool down until it is safe to open. Remove lid and blend soup in a blender, or with an immersion blender, until smooth. Add salt or Bragg's Liquid Aminos, if desired. Sprinkle with dill.

Variation: Sprinkle fresh chopped cilantro leaves instead of dill.

Serving Suggestion: Serve with cooked grains and steamed vegetables.

Mung Dhal with Carrots

Serves 6–7

Ingredients

1½ cups split mung beans (presoaked for 3-4 hours)
5 cups water
1½ tablespoons vegetable broth powder
2 tablespoons coconut oil
1 cup minced onion
A pinch of Celtic salt
2 cups carrot, peeled and cut into quarter rounds
1 teaspoon coriander powder
½ teaspoon turmeric
2 tablespoons fresh ginger root, peeled and grated
2 teaspoons fresh lemon juice
1 tablespoon Bragg's Liquid Aminos
Chopped cilantro leaves for garnish (optional)

Instructions

Place rinsed and presoaked split mung in a pressure cooker with 5 cups water and 1½ Tb vegetable broth powder.

Secure lid of pressure cooker and turn to high heat. When the pressure cooker comes to full steam, lower heat and simmer for 5 minutes (the time required will vary for different pressure cookers). Turn off heat. Let pressure cooker cool down until it is safe to open.

In a pan heat 2 tablespoons coconut oil. When the oil has heated, add 1 cup minced onion and a pinch of Celtic salt. Sauté onion until golden.

Add 2 cups quarter round carrots and continue to sauté for a few minutes. Add 1 teaspoon coriander, ½ teaspoon turmeric, 2 tablespoons grated ginger root, 2 teaspoons fresh lemon juice, and 1 tablespoon of Bragg's Liquid Aminos.

Mix well and sauté for 1 minute. Add ½ cup water, cover pan, lower heat, and simmer until water is absorbed. Turn heat off. Fold vegetable mixture with cooked split mung. If consistency of dhal is too thick, add little water and mix well.

Serving suggestion: Sprinkle fresh chopped cilantro leaves on the dhal. Serve with brown rice, steamed kale, and green beans.

Garbanzo Marinade

Serves 3–4

Ingredients

2½ cups cooked garbanzo beans (from one cup dried beans, soaked overnight and cooked the next day)
¼ cup extra-virgin olive oil
3 tablespoons Bragg's Liquid Aminos
¼ teaspoon black pepper
1 teaspoon paprika
½ cup chopped parsley

Instructions

Place 2½ cups cooked garbanzo beans in a glass bowl. Add ¼ cup extra-virgin olive oil, 3 tablespoons Bragg's, ¼ teaspoon black pepper, 1 teaspoon paprika, and ½ cup chopped parsley. Adjust seasoning as needed. Let sit for 10 to 30 minutes to absorb flavors.

Tip: Adding herbs and spices helps make garbanzo beans more digestible.

Serving Suggestion: Toss plain garbanzo beans with mixed salad greens. Add salad dressing of your choice.

Vegetables

Curried Brussels Sprouts

Serves 3–4

Ingredients

- 4 cups Brussels sprouts, rinsed, trimmed, and cut in half
- 2 tablespoons sesame oil
- 2 tablespoons sunflower oil
- 1 teaspoon Celtic salt
- ½ cup water
- 1 teaspoon coriander powder
- 1 teaspoon curry powder
- ½ teaspoon turmeric
- Bragg's Liquid Aminos

Instructions

Heat 2 tablespoons sesame oil and 2 tablespoons sunflower oil in a skillet. When the oil is well-heated, add 4 cups halved Brussels sprouts and 1 teaspoon Celtic salt. Lightly sauté. Add ½ cup water. Lower the heat and cover the pan. Allow the Brussels sprouts to steam in their juices for a few minutes.

Remove the lid and add 1 teaspoon coriander powder, 1 teaspoon curry powder, ½ teaspoon turmeric, and a drizzle of Bragg's. Cover with lid. The vegetables are done when they are soft (about 10 minutes).

Mashed Root Vegetables

Serves 4

Ingredients

- 6 cups water
- 1 teaspoon Celtic salt
- 2 red potatoes, peeled and cut into chunks
- 1 carrot, peeled and cut into chunks
- 1 turnip, peeled and cut into chunks
- 2 tablespoons extra-virgin olive oil
- 1 teaspoon sea salt
- 1 pinch black pepper
- ¼ cup minced fresh parsley

Instructions

Place 6 cups water in a pot and bring to a boil. Add 1 teaspoon Celtic salt, and 2 red potatoes, 1 carrot, and 1 turnip, all cut into chunks.

Simmer covered until the vegetables are tender (approximately 15–20 minutes, or, if using a pressure cooker, half that). Pour off the remaining water (or save as soup stock). Place the cooked vegetables in a bowl. Mash together with a fork.

Add 2 tablespoons extra-virgin olive oil, 1 teaspoon sea salt, a pinch of black pepper, and ¼ cup fresh minced parsley. Serve warm.

Serving Suggestion: Serve with green salad and black beans.

Sauces

Black Bean Sauce

Makes 2 cups

Blend in a blender:

1½ cups cooked black beans
⅓ cup cooking water from beans (to add more flavor), or plain water
2 tablespoons extra-virgin olive oil
¼ cup (packed) cilantro leaves
1 clove garlic (optional)
2 tablespoons Bragg's Liquid Aminos

Instructions

Sprinkle with fresh cilantro leaves, or parmesan cheese, as garnish.

Tip: Blending beans makes them easier to digest. Most people are familiar with hummus, which is made from blended garbanzo beans. You can make a spread or a sauce from any cooked bean.

Serving Suggestion: Serve with cooked grains and steamed vegetables.

Mung Bean Coconut Sauce

Makes 4 cups

Ingredients

1 cup mung beans (soaked overnight)
1 tablespoon coconut oil
½ cup minced onion
A pinch of Celtic salt
1 cup tomato, small cubes
½ teaspoon turmeric powder
1 teaspoon coriander powder
¼ teaspoon chili powder
1 tablespoon Bragg's Liquid Aminos

Instructions

Place in a pressure cooker soaked mung beans (drained), and 4 cups fresh water.

Secure lid of pressure cooker and turn to high heat. When the pressure cooker comes to full steam, lower the heat and simmer for 4 minutes (the time required will vary for different pressure cookers). Turn off heat. Let the pressure cooker cool down until it is safe to open. Drain beans and set aside.

In a pan, sauté 1 tablespoon coconut oil. When the oil has heated, add ½ cup minced onion and a pinch of Celtic salt. Sauté onion until golden.

Add 1 cup small cubed tomato (1 medium tomato), ½ teaspoon turmeric powder, 1 teaspoon coriander powder, ¼ teaspoon chili powder, and 1 tablespoon of Bragg's Liquid Aminos. Mix and simmer for a few minutes. Then add to pan 1 cup coconut milk and cooked mung beans. Simmer for a few minutes to mix flavors. Turn off heat and serve.

Serving Suggestion: Serve with cooked rice or quinoa, and steamed carrots and kale.

Zucchini-Carrot Sauce

Makes 2 cups

Ingredients

2 tablespoons sunflower oil
1 medium onion, minced
A few pinches of Celtic salt
1 medium carrot, peeled and cut into quarter rounds
2 medium zucchini, cut into half rounds
2 tablespoons extra-virgin olive oil
3 tablespoons whole wheat pastry flour or garbanzo flour (gluten-free)
¾ cup water
1 teaspoon sea salt, or to taste
⅛ teaspoon black pepper, or to taste

Instructions

Put 2 tablespoons sunflower oil in a skillet and sauté 1 medium onion, minced, with a pinch of Celtic salt, until the onions are golden. Add 1 medium carrot, peeled and cut into quarter rounds, and sauté for 5 minutes, stirring frequently.

Add 2 medium zucchini, cut into half rounds, a bit more Celtic salt, and 2 tablespoons extra-virgin olive oil, and sauté for another 5 minutes, or until the vegetables are soft.

Sprinkle 3 tablespoons of whole wheat pastry flour, coating the vegetables to give this sauce its thickness and gravy-like consistency. Stir in ¾ cup water. Cook on low heat for another 3–5 minutes. Stir frequently to prevent burning.

When done, remove from pan and blend in a food processor (or use a hand blender) until smooth. Add 1 teaspoon salt and ⅛ teaspoon black pepper, or add to taste.

Serving Suggestion: Serve with basmati rice and legumes such as black beans.

Green Sauce

Makes 1 cup

Blend in a blender:

½ cup extra-virgin olive oil
½ cup (packed) cilantro leaves
½ cup (packed) parsley leaves
A pinch of sea salt

Sprinkle a few cilantro leaves. Keep refrigerated.

Serving Suggestion: Mix and serve Green Sauce with grains, to help moisten them.

Orange-Cashew Sauce

Makes 1¼ cups

Ingredients

1 cup raw cashew pieces
1 cup fresh orange juice (2–3 oranges)
2 tablespoons extra-virgin olive oil

Instructions

Put in a blender 1 cup raw cashew pieces. Grind on high speed until a fine powder is created. Transfer the powder to a small bowl. Blend in the blender until creamy: 1 cup fresh orange juice, 2 tablespoons extra-virgin olive oil, and cashew powder (add last).

Variation: When in season, use tangerine juice instead of orange juice.

Serving Suggestion: Pour this sauce on steamed vegetables, cooked grains, or legumes. It is especially tasty on cooked black beans.

Orange-Ginger Sauce

Makes ½ cup

Mix in a Bowl

¼ cup fresh orange juice
2 tablespoons fresh lemon juice
1 tablespoon maple syrup
1½ teaspoons fresh ginger root juice

Keep refrigerated.

Serving Suggestion: Pour this sauce on a salad of grated beets and toasted walnuts, with a garnish of fresh cilantro.

Lemon Herb Sauce

Makes ⅔ cup

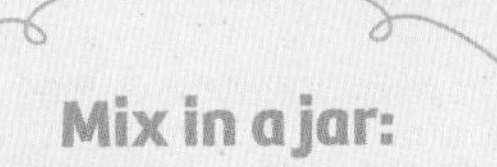

Mix in a jar:

6 tablespoons extra-virgin olive oil
2 tablespoons lemon juice
1 tablespoon minced basil
1 tablespoon minced parsley
1 tablespoon minced oregano
1 tablespoon minced mint

Tip: The more finely you chop the fresh herbs, the more intense the flavor.

Serving Suggestion: Pour over veggies, grains, and beans. Serve with salad.

Tahini-Dill Dressing

Makes 1¾ cups

Blend until smooth:

¾ cup fresh water
(2–3 tablespoons less for thicker consistency)
¼ cup extra-virgin olive oil
¼ cup fresh lemon juice
½ cup tahini (organic, roasted)
1 tablespoon maple syrup, or a pinch of stevia powder
2 teaspoons tamari or Bragg's Liquid Aminos
½ teaspoon garlic powder
½ teaspoon dill weed
¼ teaspoon salt
1 pinch black pepper

Serving Suggestion: This light, summery dressing is sweet and refreshing on green salad. It also goes well with plain basmati white rice, steamed kale and carrot, and plain garbanzo beans. Keep refrigerated.

Tahini-Ginger Dressing

Makes 1¾ cups

Blend until smooth:

1–2 cloves of garlic, minced
2 tablespoons fresh ginger root, peeled and grated
¼ cup extra-virgin olive oil
1½ tablespoons sesame oil
¼ cup fresh lemon juice
¼ cup tamari or Bragg's Liquid Aminos
⅓ cup tahini (organic, roasted)

Tip: This dressing contains olive oil, which may harden when refrigerated. To soften the oil, place the container in hot water for a few minutes before serving. Or take the dressing out of the fridge half an hour before use to bring it to room temperature. Keep refrigerated.

Vitality Dressing

Makes 2 cups

Instructions

In a blender place 2 cups extra-virgin olive oil or sunflower oil, and ½ cup tamari or Bragg's Liquid Aminos. Add and pulse 4 teaspoons prepared Dijon mustard.

Add dry herbs to blender and blend on low speed for one minute: 2 teaspoons ground coriander, 2 teaspoons powdered ginger, 2 teaspoons powdered cumin, 2 teaspoons dried basil, 2 teaspoons dried dill, 3 teaspoons granulated onion. Keep refrigerated.

Tips: • To ensure that the dry ingredients mix fully with the liquid, first blend the liquid ingredients, then add the dry Ingredients.

• If using olive oil, this dressing may harden when refrigerated. To soften the oil, place the container in hot water for a few minutes before serving.

Ingredients

- 2 cups extra-virgin olive oil or sunflower oil
- ½ cup tamari or Bragg's Liquid Aminos
- 4 teaspoons prepared Dijon mustard
- 2 teaspoons ground coriander
- 2 teaspoons powdered ginger
- 2 teaspoons powdered cumin
- 2 teaspoons dried basil
- 2 teaspoons dried dill
- 3 teaspoons granulated onion

Miso Dressing

Makes 1 cup

Blend until smooth:

- ½ cup sunflower oil
- 1 tablespoon sesame oil
- 2 tablespoons fresh lemon juice
- ¼ cup fresh water
- 2 tablespoons mellow miso
- 1 tablespoon fresh ginger root, peeled and grated, or 1 teaspoon fresh ginger root juice*

Keep refrigerated.

Variation for an oil-free Miso Dressing (Makes ½ cup)

Blend until smooth:

- 1½ tablespoons mellow miso
- 1 tablespoon fresh lemon juice
- 1 tablespoon fresh ginger root, peeled and grated
- ¼ cup fresh water

Serving Suggestion: This light summery dressing is sweet and refreshing on green salad. It is also a lovely sauce on plain basmati white rice, on steamed kale and carrot, and on plain garbanzo beans.

Keep refrigerated.

*See glossary for how to make ginger juice.

Lemon-Ginger Dressing

Makes 2 ½ cups

Blend until smooth:

1 cup sunflower oil
⅔ cup fresh lemon juice
6 tablespoons tamari or Bragg's Liquid Aminos
3 tablespoons sunflower seeds
⅓ cup water
2 tablespoons fresh ginger root, peeled and grated
2 teaspoons dry mustard
2 cloves garlic, peeled (optional)

Serving Suggestion: This robust, crowd-pleasing dressing accents any dish. Keep refrigerated.

Every day is a special occasion
*when you have **good friends***

Part 6: *Appendices, and More*

Glossary

Aduki beans: Also called adzuki or azuki beans.

Arrowroot: A natural starch flour, used as a thickening agent, similar to cornstarch. It gives a stickier and more gelatinous texture than cornstarch. Arrowroot is a particularly good thickening agent for liquids and dishes that have delicate flavors.

Buckwheat noodle: A buckwheat flour noodle, also called soba noodle. If you are allergic to wheat, you can use buckwheat, which is gluten free.

Chia seeds: Edible seeds with a mild, nutty flavor. Chia seeds can be sprinkled on cereals, sauces, vegetables, and rice dishes, and added to smoothies. They are a good source of fiber, healthy omega-3 fats, and an aid to digestion.

Dulse: A red sea vegetable that is mildly spicy and salty in flavor.

Edamame: Young green soybeans. It is best to use fresh edamame, but if you can't find fresh ones, use frozen edamame. They make a healthy snack.

Garam masala: A blend of ground spices commonly used in Indian and Asian cuisines. Pungent, but not hot in the same way as chili pepper, it will generally include cloves, cumin, cinnamon, cardamom, nutmeg, anise, and coriander.

Ghee: Clarified butter—butter from which the milk solids have been removed. Ghee has a sweet, light taste and is easier to digest than butter. In India it has been used for centuries as one of the most effective ways to absorb a variety of Ayurvedic medicines. (See page 254 for instructions on how to make ghee.)

Green Magma: A powdered barley-grass juice. It contains an abundance of vitamins, minerals, amino acids, proteins, and chlorophyll.

Hemp protein powder: A rich plant source of protein. It contains a wide range of amino acids, as well as omega fatty acids high in dietary fiber, and is easy to digest.

Kamut: A form of wheat from the Mediterranean. It's about two or three times the size of modern wheat. Kamut contains high levels of protein and minerals. People with wheat sensitivity can enjoy this grain with no allergic reaction.

Kombu: An edible seaweed kelp.

Miso: A paste made from fermented soybeans that can be mixed with grains such as rice or barley. There are several varieties of miso, which vary in saltiness and strength.

The choice of the miso paste will define the flavor of the dish. White Miso (mellow miso) has a mild, sweet flavor. Red and brown miso have a strong earthy flavor. If you are just starting to use miso, try first the white miso, with its mellow and sweet taste. Because miso is a living food containing many beneficial microorganisms that are diminished by overcooking, it is recommended to add it to food just before the food is removed from the heat. Miso needs to be refrigerated.

Nori: A Japanese name for an edible seaweed sheet. To make nori rolls, it's best to use toasted nori sheets. You can cut a nori sheet into small pieces to eat as a snack or sprinkle over soup.

Seitan: A wheat gluten, made from whole wheat flour and water. It has a chewy, meatlike texture. You can find it ready-made at natural food stores, but homemade seitan is less expensive and tastes better. To make it at home, you need to buy wheat gluten flour (also called vital wheat gluten) at your local natural food store. See how to make seitan in section 2, winter meal 5.

Quinoa: A whole grain that is a complete protein and gluten free. The skin of the quinoa seed is quite bitter, so it's best to rinse it a few times before cooking it.

Tahini: A paste made from ground sesame seeds.

Udon: A wheat flour noodle.

Wakame: An edible seaweed, used in salads and soups.

Wheat berry: A whole wheat kernel (grain).

Whey: A liquid byproduct of cheese manufacturing. While most people can tolerate whey protein, those with lactose intolerance or milk allergies may experience gas or bloating after ingestion.

Xylitol: A natural sweetener from the birch tree.

How to Make Ginger Juice

Grate fresh whole unpeeled ginger root. Place a small amount of grated ginger at a time into the palm of your hand, and squeeze the juice into a bowl. Discard the ginger pulp. Or use a garlic press: place grated unpeeled ginger in the press and squeeze the juice into a bowl.

How to Make Ghee

Ghee is an ideal cooking oil, as it does not burn unless heated excessively. It is used instead of butter and keeps without refrigeration. People who are allergic to dairy products and are unable to enjoy butter may be able to tolerate ghee.

Commercial ghee is available at health food stores and Indian groceries, but it's easy and more economical to make your own.

The preparation time is about 40–50 minutes. You will need a flame diffuser* and a timer.

Instructions

In a heavy saucepan (preferably stainless steel), place **1 pound unsalted butter** (regular or raw). Melt the butter and cook over medium to low heat (best to use a flame diffuser if possible) so that the butter just boils gently. Do not cover the pot.

A foam of milk solids will rise to the surface; do not skim off or stir.

After about 30–40 minutes the foam will settle to the bottom of the pot, where it will create a thick layer. At this point watch the ghee carefully to avoid burning. When the bottom layer turns a light tan color and the liquid becomes clear and golden, the ghee has formed.

Remove from heat and let cool. Pour the contents of the pot through a fine sieve into a glass container for storage.

Note: After the ghee is done and has cooled, keep it covered and avoid using a wet spoon, or allowing any water to mix with it, as that will create the conditions for bacteria to grow and spoil the ghee. Burnt ghee has a nutty smell and a brownish color; it can still be used if not burned excessively.

* A flame diffuser is a ring or round device that is placed on the stove's heating element or burner to separate the cooking pan from the heat source (similar to a wok ring).

Nine-Day Cleansing and Vitalizing Diet

The Nine-Day Cleansing and Vitalizing Diet* has proven a most effective method for ridding the system of poisons.

Yogananda called this diet "a method for rejuvenating the body cells and awakening the latent powers of the mind and the inner forces of the soul."

* Be sure to check with a medical professional before doing this diet, which is not appropriate for people on blood thinners, nor for those who are pregnant, nor for those with diabetes.

The Nine-Day Cleansing Diet consists of the following daily foods:

- 1½ grapefruits
- 5 oranges
- 1½ lemons
- 1 raw vegetable salad
- 1 cooked vegetable with juice (quantity optional)
- 3 cups Vitality Beverage (one at each meal)
- 1 glass orange juice with a teaspoon of senna leaves or Original Swiss Kriss. (To be taken every night during the cleansing diet, before going to bed. To obtain the best results, take ½ teaspoon at first; later, increase to 1 teaspoon.)

Vitality Beverage Ingredients:

- 2 stalks chopped celery
- 1 bunch chopped parsley
- 1 quart water (4 cups)
- 2 cups chopped spinach, dandelion, or turnip greens
- No salt or spices
- 5 carrots (chopped), including part of the stems

The beverage may be prepared in two ways; the first way is preferable:

1. After putting celery and carrots through a food processor, or chopping them finely, lightly boil them in water for ten minutes. Then add the leafy greens and parsley and boil ten minutes longer. Strain by squeezing through a cheesecloth.
2. Use the same ingredients, but do not cook them. Put them through a vegetable juicer.

The vitality beverage is essential to the cleansing action of the diet. Drink one cup of the beverage at each of the three meals. This vitality beverage has been found to be a blood tonic and a very effective aid for rheumatism, various stomach disorders (including acute indigestion), chronic catarrh, bronchitis, and nervous strain.

While on the cleansing diet, strictly abstain from spices, candies, pastries, meat, eggs, fish, cheese, milk, butter, bread, fried foods, oil, beans—in fact, all foods not specific to the diet.

If one feels a need for additional nourishment, take one tablespoonful of thoroughly ground nuts in half a glass of water or in a glass of orange juice.

After the Nine-Day Diet, you should be especially careful in the selection and quantity of your food for at least four days, and resume your normal diet gradually. Begin by adding a portion of cottage cheese to your meal. Almonds, egg yolk, and baked potato are among the first foods to be added. Do not overeat. Gradually increase the amount and variety until you are again on a normal diet.

If you are unsuccessful in ridding the body of all poisons during the initial attempt, repeat the cleansing diet after two or three weeks.

Before going to bed every night while on the diet, it has been found beneficial to soak in two pounds of Epsom salts in one-quarter tub of warm water. It is also very helpful to take a salts bath every now and then for several weeks after finishing the diet.

Tips about the cleansing diet

- You may experience irritability the first few days.
- Sometimes people have headaches in the beginning, especially those who habitually drink coffee or black tea. The headaches seem to be caused by caffeine withdrawal.
- You may also find a psychological change in your attitude toward food. Although you are actually eating large quantities, because the food is without salt, oil, or seasonings of any kind, it doesn't provide the sensory satisfaction we usually get. You may find yourself not interested in food at all.

A few helpful suggestions

- Take regular sunbaths, exposing as much of the body as possible to direct sunlight. Yogananda said that you can receive up to ten times the benefit from solar energy if you consciously draw the sun's energy into your body cells.
- The Nine-Day Diet is easiest to complete during the spring or summer months, which seems to be a natural cleansing time for the body. Also, because of the decreased caloric intake, the body tends to feel cold during the diet, which is less of a problem during warm weather. In the spring and summer, there is also a greater variety of fresh vegetables available for steaming.

A suggested regime for daily food consumption

- Breakfast—grapefruits and vitality beverage
- Lunch—salad and vitality beverage
- Dinner—steamed vegetables, lemons, and vitality beverage
- Oranges eaten throughout the day
- Experiment and find what works best for you.
- When coming off the diet, eat lightly and simply for the first few days.

Measures and Weights Conversion

Measuring cups and spoons are an essential part of successful cooking. As you become more experienced in using them, you will be able to calculate and multiply without needing a chart. It is helpful and useful to know, for example, how many teaspoons equal one tablespoon, or how many tablespoons are in one cup.

Note: When measuring, assume all cup and spoon measures are level, unless otherwise stated (e.g. rounded, heaped).

1 pinch = less than ⅛ teaspoon (dry)

1 dash = 3 drops to ¼ teaspoon (liquid)

1 tablespoon = 3 teaspoons = ½ fl. ounce (liquid ounce)

¼ cup = 4 tablespoons

⅓ cup = 5 tablespoons + 1 teaspoon

½ cup = 8 tablespoons

¾ cup = 12 tablespoons

1 cup = 16 tablespoons

1 cup = ½ pint = 8 fl. oz.

1 pint = 2 cups = ½ quart = 16 fl. oz. = 32 tablespoons

1 quart = 4 cups = 2 pints = ¼ gallon = 32 fl. oz.

1 gallon = 16 cups = 8 pints = 4 quarts = 128 fl. oz.

16 ounces (oz.) = 1 pound (abbreviated as lb. or #)

Herbs and Spices Measure: 1 tablespoon fresh herb = 1 teaspoon dry herb

Abbreviations: tablespoon = Tbs. teaspoon = tsp.

Converting to Natural Ingredients (Substitutions)

1 cup sugar	=	¾ cup maple syrup, and delete ¼ cup liquid from the recipe
	=	1 cup Sucanat
	=	1 cup xylitol
	=	¾ cup Sucanat + ¼ cup maple syrup minus 1 Tbs. liquid
	=	1¼ cups date sugar + ¼ cup maple syrup
1 cup honey	=	⅓ cup maple syrup + ⅓ cup rice syrup + ⅓ cup water
	=	¾ cup amazake + ¼ cup liquid
1 cup molasses	=	½ cup barley malt + ½ cup maple syrup heated together
1 cup liquid sweetener	=	1–3 drops stevia (honey leaf)
1 cup white flour	=	1 cup whole wheat flour, whole wheat pastry flour, corn flour, barley flour, or oat flour
	=	1 cup gluten-free flour (brown rice flour, tapioca flour, potato flour, garbanzo flour)
1 large egg	=	3 Tbs. soy milk/nut milk
	=	1 Tbs. flax seed ground into powder, then blended with ¼ cup water until gluey
	=	1 Tbs. arrowroot + 1 Tbs. soy flour + 2 Tbs. water
	=	½ tsp. baking powder
	=	½ cup mashed banana/potato/sweet potato
1 egg yolk	=	1 Tbs. + 1 tsp. liquid
1 egg white	=	2 Tbs. liquid
1 cup butter	=	¾ cup + 2½ tsp. oil
Coffee	=	Cafix, Inka, Pero (1:1 ratio)
1 cup milk	=	1 cup soy milk, rice milk, nut milk, fruit juice + 2 Tbs. oil (1:1 ratio)
1 cup buttermilk	=	1 cup soy milk + 2 tsp. lemon juice
	=	¾ cup yogurt + ¼ cup water
1 tsp. salt	=	2 Tbs. miso
	=	4 Tbs. tamari

Index

About the Author

For many years Diksha McCord was the head chef at The Expanding Light (Expandinglight.org), Ananda's retreat center.

She learned vegetarian cooking while growing up in Israel. Later she lived in Japan, where she became familiar with Japanese cuisine, and then in California, where she explored macrobiotic, vegan, and Ayurvedic cooking.

Diksha is the author of two other cookbooks: *Global Kitchen* and *Vegetarian Cooking for Starters*. She created and hosts Online Vegetarian Cooking for Health and Vitality, a four-season video series.

A resident since 1993 of Ananda Village, a spiritual cooperative community in the foothills of the Sierra Nevada mountains in Northern California, Diksha serves as a minister and teacher at The Expanding Light, where she also directs the Ananda Meditation® Teacher Training. In addition, she and her husband, Gyandev, lead workshops in many locations around the world.

After receiving her BS in Biology from Hebrew University, she spent four years in medical research. Later she earned her BFA from Israel's Bezalel Academy of Arts and Design, and received numerous awards for her work. Diksha also spent three years in a master's program at Kyoto Art University in Japan.

Online Cooking Course

Vegetarian Cooking for Health and Vitality

with Diksha McCord

Watch this cookbook come alive through the online course! You will enjoy meeting Diksha "in person" for step-by-step instructions in cooking many delicious recipes. With easy-to-find ingredients and simple recipes, the results will be delightful and satisfying for you and your guests.

Included in your Full-Year Subscription, you'll receive 1 year access to:

- 47 short Cooking Basics videos
- 22 Basic Recipes
- 6 Introductory Articles
- Your Vegetarian Kitchen

Access any portion of the course anytime you wish—and revisit as often as you like!

PLUS

Four Seasons' Meals & Specials

- Videos of 32 complete meals
- 16 specials

For more information, please visit us at:
http://www.expandinglight.org/online-learning/vegetarian-cooking/

A Special Taste for our readers!

Enjoy cooking with higher awareness with Diksha. As a gift to go along with this book, we're offering access to all four Holiday Meal video classes for free:
THANKSGIVING, CHRISTMAS, EASTER,
AND FOURTH OF JULY ~ *Bon Appetit!*

www.onlinewithananda.org/holidaymeals

Ananda

Dear Reader,

Ananda is a worldwide work based on the same teachings expressed in this book—those of the great spiritual teacher, Paramhansa Yogananda. If you enjoyed this title, Crystal Clarity Publishers invites you to continue to deepen your spiritual life through the many avenues of Ananda Worldwide—including meditation communities, centers, and groups; online virtual community and webinars; retreat centers offering classes and teacher training in yoga and meditation; and more.

For special offers and discounts for first-time visitors to Ananda, visit: **www.crystalclarity.com/welcome**. Feel free to contact us. We are here to serve you.

Joy to you,
Crystal Clarity Publishers

ANANDA WORLDWIDE

Ananda, a worldwide organization founded by Swami Kriyananda, offers spiritual support and resources based on the teachings of Paramhansa Yogananda. There are Ananda spiritual communities in Nevada City, Sacramento, and Palo Alto, California; Seattle, Washington; Portland and Laurelwood, Oregon; as well as a retreat center and European community in Assisi, Italy, and a community near New Delhi, India. Ananda supports more than 140 meditation groups worldwide.

For more information about Ananda's work, our communities, or meditation groups near you, please call 530.478.7560 or visit **www.ananda.org.**

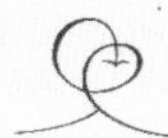

THE EXPANDING LIGHT

The Expanding Light is the largest retreat center in the world to share exclusively the teachings of Paramhansa Yogananda. Situated in the Ananda Village community, it offers the opportunity to experience spiritual life in a contemporary ashram setting. The varied, year-round schedule of classes and programs on yoga, meditation, and spiritual practice includes Karma Yoga, Personal Retreat, Spiritual Travel, and online learning. The Ananda School of Yoga & Meditation offers certified yoga, yoga therapist, spiritual counselor, and meditation teacher trainings. Large groups are welcome.

The teaching staff are experts in Kriya Yoga meditation and all aspects of Yogananda's teachings. All staff members live at Ananda Village and bring an uplifting approach to their areas of service. The serene natural setting and delicious vegetarian meals help provide an ideal environment for a truly meaningful visit.

For more information, please call 800.346.5350 or visit **www.expandinglight.org.**

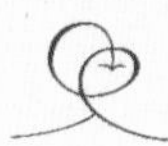

CRYSTAL CLARITY PUBLISHERS

Crystal Clarity Publishers offers many additional resources to assist you in your spiritual journey, including many other books (see the following pages for some of them), a wide variety of inspirational and relaxation music composed by Swami Kriyananda, and yoga and meditation videos. To request a catalog, place an order for the above products, or to find out more information, please contact us at:

Crystal Clarity Publishers / **www.crystalclarity.com**
14618 Tyler Foote Rd. / Nevada City, CA 95959
TOLL FREE: 800.424.1055 or 530.478.7600 / FAX: 530.478.7610
EMAIL: clarity@crystalclarity.com
For our online catalog, complete with secure ordering, please visit our website.

Further Explorations

GLOBAL KITCHEN

A Cookbook of Vegetarian Favorites from The Expanding Light Retreat
Diksha McCord

Create healthy, flavorful meals with an international flair! The delicious, easy-to-prepare recipes in *Global Kitchen* are inspired by many of the world's most-enjoyed culinary cultures—Italian, Thai, Indian, and Chinese, among others.

Diksha McCord was the head chef at The Expanding Light retreat for seven years, where she now teaches vegetarian cooking classes. She learned Kosher and vegetarian cooking while growing up in Israel, studied Japanese cooking while living in Kyoto, Japan, and learned Ayurvedic and Indian cooking from premier California chefs.

VEGETARIAN COOKING FOR STARTERS

Simple Recipes & Techniques for Health and Vitality
Diksha McCord

Are you confused by the many different foods, theories, fads, and techniques championed by various proponents of healthy eating? This book gives straightforward, easy-to-follow dietary advice, explains what common vegetarian foods are, offers useful explanations on how to prepare vegetarian dishes, and includes simple, savory recipes that will help you add vegetarian meals to your diet.

Most importantly, these low-fat recipes are delicious! So whether you'd like to become a complete vegetarian, incorporate some vegetarian eating into your current diet, or just learn how to cook vegetarian food for a loved one, this book is for you.

SIMPLY VEGETARIAN

Easy-to-Prepare Recipes for the Vegetarian Gourmet
Nancy Mair

Gourmet easy-to-prepare vegetarian dishes! A winning combination that includes 50 main dishes as well as a whole selection of soups, salads, and stunning desserts for a complete meal. This cookbook appeals to everyone, both vegetarian and non-vegetarian, whether family or guests. Completely revised, new recipes reflect the most current trends in gourmet cooking.

In this age of greater awareness about the need for more balance in our diet, *Simply Vegetarian!* offers meatless meals of superior taste. Easy-to-find ingredients and reasonable preparation times accommodate the schedule of the busiest cooks. The dishes, rich in taste and texture, please even the most sophisticated palate.

The original 1946 unedited edition of Yogananda's spiritual masterpiece

AUTOBIOGRAPHY OF A YOGI

Paramhansa Yogananda

Also in audiobook MP3

Autobiography of a Yogi is one of the best-selling Eastern philosophy titles of all time, with millions of copies sold, named one of the best and most influential books of the twentieth century. This highly prized reprinting of the original 1946 edition is the only one available free from textual changes made after Yogananda's death. Yogananda was the first yoga master of India whose mission was to live and teach in the West. In this updated edition are bonus materials, including a last chapter that Yogananda wrote in 1951, without posthumous changes.

"In the original edition, published during Yogananda's life, one is more in contact with Yogananda himself. While Yogananda founded centers and organizations, his concern was more with guiding individuals to direct communion with Divinity rather than with promoting any one church as opposed to another. This spirit is easier to grasp in the original edition of this great spiritual and yogic classic." —***David Frawley,*** *Director, American Institute of Vedic Studies, author of* Yoga and Ayurveda

THE NEW PATH

My Life with Paramhansa Yogananda

Swami Kriyananda

Winner of the 2010 Eric Hoffer Award for Best Self-Help/Spiritual Book

Winner of the 2010 USA Book News Award for Best Spiritual Book

This is the moving story of Kriyananda's years with Paramhansa Yogananda, India's emissary to the West and the first yoga master to spend the greater part of his life in America. When Swami Kriyananda discovered *Autobiography of a Yogi* in 1948, he was totally new to Eastern teachings. This is a great advantage to the Western reader, since Kriyananda walks us along the yogic path as he discovers it from the moment of his initiation as a disciple of Yogananda. With winning honesty, humor, and deep insight, he shares his journey on the spiritual path through personal stories and experiences.

PARAMHANSA YOGANANDA

A Biography, with Personal Reflections and Reminiscences

Swami Kriyananda

Paramhansa Yogananda's classic *Autobiography of a Yogi* is more about the saints Yogananda met than about himself—in spite of Yogananda's astonishing accomplishments. Now, one of Yogananda's direct disciples relates the untold story of this great spiritual master and world teacher: his teenage miracles, his challenges in coming to America, his national lecture campaigns, his struggles to fulfill his world-changing mission amid incomprehension and painful betrayals, and his ultimate triumphant achievement. Kriyananda's subtle grasp of his guru's inner nature reveals Yogananda's many-sided greatness. Includes many never-before-published anecdotes.

HOW TO MEDITATE

A Step-by-Step Guide to the Art & Science of Meditation
Jyotish Novak

This clear and concise guidebook contains everything you need to start your practice. With easy-to-follow instructions, meditation teacher Jyotish Novak demystifies meditation—presenting the essential techniques so that you can quickly grasp them. Since it was first published in 1989, *How to Meditate* has helped thousands establish a regular meditation routine. This newly revised edition includes a bonus chapter on scientific studies showing the benefits of meditation, plus all-new photographs and illustrations.

"Meditation is a complicated term for something that is truly simple. *How To Meditate* is a guide to mastering meditation and reaping more of the benefit of the serenity of the matter. With tips on finding relaxation, opening your natural intuition, and more, this book is a must for those who want to unlock their spirituality." —*Midwest Book Review*

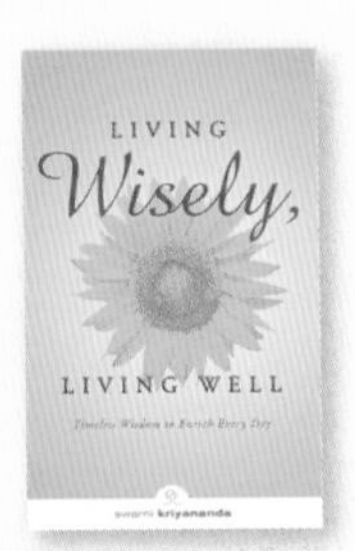

LIVING WISELY, LIVING WELL

Swami Kriyananda

Want to transform your life? Tap into your highest potential? Get inspired, uplifted, and motivated? This book contains 366 practical ways to improve your life—a thought for each day of the year. Each reading is warm with wisdom, alive with positive expectation, and provides simple actions that bring profound results. See life with new eyes. Discover hundreds of techniques for self-improvement.

DECEMBER 12

Include the success of *others* in your efforts to succeed, yourself. Better a stream that makes green a whole valley than an oasis surrounded by vast stretches of sand.

SPIRITUAL YOGA

Awakening to Higher Awareness
Gyandev McCord

Imagine that you've hired Michelangelo to repaint your kitchen cabinets. Plain white. No doubt he would do a great job, but might you be missing out on something much better? It's the same with hatha yoga, which is above all a tool for spiritual growth. Many practitioners are missing its higher purpose: to help you raise your consciousness and achieve ever-greater happiness.

Based on the teachings of Paramhansa Yogananda, this wonderful book includes: the mind-energy-body connection; the art of meditation; spiritualizing yoga postures; spiritual yoga routines; affirmations and energy control suggestions; mastering pranayama (energy control); and breathing exercises for greater energy, calmness, and concentration.